NO ADULT LEFT BEHIND

AI is Learning. Are you?

Written by

George Pillari

RUNNING FOX PARTNERS

ISBN: 9798195157883

Printed in the United States of America

Mentors help you find your North Star, and I have had some good ones. Thank you.

Tommy, Carl, Billy, Steve, Phil, Rick, and Guy

Table of Contents

- 6 -

INTRODUCTION

The future is already here; it's just not evenly distributed.

~ William Gibson, novelist.

An AI story

A few months ago, I was at a friend's house helping him install some audio equipment. We spent the better part of an hour plugging things in, reading labels, swapping cables, and making a mess of it. My friend, who is a smart, successful guy who has navigated his career with skill and confidence for decades, was getting frustrated. We were stuck.

So, I did what I thought any normal person would do. I took out my phone, snapped a picture of the back panel of the receiver, and uploaded it to ChatGPT. I asked the AI to troubleshoot the problem and suggest solutions. In a few seconds, it came back with four specific, clearly explained actions to test. After the first choice did not work, we tried the second one. The system worked perfectly.

My friend stood there for a moment and stared at me. He looked staggered, not by the AI, but by the nonchalance with which I had used it. No fanfare. No "watch this." Just a quick photo and a question, the same way you'd ask a knowledgeable friend standing next to you.

That moment stuck with me.

My friend is not a foolish man. He is accomplished, experienced, and well-regarded in his field. But in that moment, this tool, which was something I had been efficiently using every day, was something he had been watching from a distance, meaning to get around to one day. He had been observing AI the way you observe a neighbor's renovation project: mildly curious, vaguely impressed, but not your problem right now.

That is what this book is about.

There is a split happening in the professional world. The split is quiet, and in some ways, more consequential than what happens in your bank account. On one side are people who have learned to use AI as a daily instrument. They are not experts, but are habitual users. They reach for it the way a previous generation reached for a calculator, a spreadsheet, or a search engine. On the other side are people who know AI exists, believe it is probably important, and intend to learn more about it when things settle down a little.

I don't know why or when things will settle down.

I have another friend who got it right from the beginning. He sent me a long, detailed dialogue he had saved from a research session with an AI engine. What struck me was not the content of the conversation, but the way he was conducting it. He was using complete sentences and proper grammar. When the AI gave him a useful answer, he responded with, "Thank you, but can you go deeper on that last point?" He was treating the AI the way you would treat a brilliant research assistant who was sitting across the table. My friend was confident that the quality of his questions would determine the quality of the answers.

Friend #2, as I think of him, totally gets it. He understands intuitively that AI is not a search engine with better marketing. It is not a magic answer machine. It is a tool that amplifies your thinking in proportion to how well you have learned to use it.

This distinction matters enormously, and it is the beating heart of this book.

We have been here before, though perhaps not quite like this. Think back to the early days of the personal computer, when most offices had one of them, and it belonged to the person who seemed to enjoy suffering. Then came the spreadsheet, and suddenly the people who learned to use it became indispensable. The spreadsheet's users could calculate numbers in seconds, a task that previously took days by hand. The analysts who mastered these tools did not just work faster. They thought differently. They could ask questions that were previously unanswerable because the effort of answering them was prohibitive.

Then came email. Then the internet. At each inflection point, there was a cohort of people who adopted early, a larger cohort who followed in the middle, and a trailing group that resisted, sometimes for years. I have known people who refused to use email well into the 2000s because they had a perfectly good phone. I have known people who dismissed the internet as a fad with no real business application. In every case, the world did not wait for them to be ready.

In the last twenty years, I am not sure a person could land an interview for a serious business role without at least a working familiarity with Excel. It became a baseline, not because Excel is the most important skill a businessperson can have, but because it became the lingua franca of quantitative thinking in the workplace. If you did not speak it, you were signaling something about your willingness to adapt. AI is in this category, except it is moving way faster than the spreadsheet ever did.

The difference this time is the speed of the wave. It took roughly fifteen years for email to go from novelty to universal expectation in the professional world. The trajectory for AI is compressed to a fraction of that time. The people who are "getting around to it" may find that by the time they do, the gap between them and their AI-fluent peers has widened considerably.

The word I keep returning to is augmentation. To augment something is to increase its value or quality by adding to it. A calculator does not replace your ability to think about numbers, but it removes the friction of arithmetic so that you can think about numbers at a higher level. AI works the same way, only the ceiling is much higher and the range of tasks it can touch is vastly wider.

Consider the business presentation. You have two pages of rough notes, a few bullet points, some data you jotted down after a meeting, and the vague outline of an argument. You need to stand up in front of senior leadership in a week and make a compelling, professional, and well-structured case. For most people, the distance between the raw material and the finished product is where things fall apart. Not because they lack ideas, but because translating ideas into polished output under time pressure is hard.

Take the notes, the data, the scribbled diagram, and hand them to an AI with a clear prompt. Ask it to create a ten-minute presentation that highlights the most relevant points for senior management, using the company's color scheme, organized around a clear narrative arc. What comes back will not be perfect. But it will be a serious first draft. It will be structured and will have caught things you buried in your notes. In three minutes, it will have done what might otherwise take you three hours.

This book was born out of a newsletter series called "Learning AI," published on my website, theCautionary.com. The premise was simple: take real questions, the kind that ordinary, intelligent adults have about their lives and careers, and decisions, and put them to the leading AI engines. Publish the actual conversations. Show the results. Let the reader see not just what AI said, but how to ask it the right things in the first place.

The questions ranged from the practical to the philosophical. Can AI help me prepare for a job interview? Can it pick stocks that beat the market? How does the AI inside a self-driving car decide what to do when there is no good option? Could AI have prevented the *Titanic* from sinking? How should AI be used in warfare? What career should I point my kids toward in a world where AI can do so many jobs?

Each experiment was a lesson, not just in what AI could do, but in how to think about it. The series attracted readers who were curious but not yet committed, but who sensed that AI was important, but were not sure where to begin, or whether it was really for them.

This book is for the experienced professional who is wondering whether the window to get on board is closing. It is for the mid-career adult who watched the internet wave and the smartphone wave and caught those without too much trouble, but senses that this one is different. It is for the parent trying to give their child honest advice about what skills will matter. It is for anyone who has a nagging feeling that they should use these tools more but is not entirely sure how.

The title of this book is a provocation, but it is also a sincere plea.

No Child Left Behind was a U.S. education policy from 2001 premised on the idea that every child deserved access to the tools and opportunities that would allow them to succeed. Whatever one thinks of the policy itself, the instinct behind it was right: when a transformational shift happens, you do not want the least-equipped members of society to be the ones who miss it entirely.

The AI shift is transformational in exactly that way. And unlike some technological shifts that primarily affect a narrow slice of the population, this one touches nearly every profession, every industry, and every level of an organization. The lawyer who uses AI to review contracts. The nurse who uses it to keep up with medical literature. The small business owner who uses it to draft marketing copy, answer customer questions, and analyze inventory. The job applicant who uses it to prepare and to present himself. The retiree who uses it to decipher a confusing insurance document or troubleshoot an uncooperative smart television.

The stakes are not evenly distributed. People in mid- and late career who have built real expertise, real judgment, and wisdom over decades are at particular risk of being stranded by this wave if they do not engage with it deliberately. Not because they are less capable, but because the urgency is less obvious to them. They have succeeded without AI. They have, as my friend does, a comfortable distance from which to observe.

I am asking them (that means you) to close that distance.

Not to become an expert, not to write code, or not to understand how large language models work at a technical level. Simply to begin. To take a picture of the back of that appliance panel and ask a question. To upload your notes and see what comes back. To treat the AI the way Friend #2 does: as a capable, tireless, extraordinarily well-read assistant who is available at any hour and who will meet you where you are.

This book is divided into three parts: Getting Started, AI and Careers, and AI in Daily Life.

The "Getting Started" chapters discuss the differences between using search and using AI, the fine art of prompting, and how to make AI your friend when confronted with complex documents. If you are already an avid AI user, skim through this section.

The chapters on Careers focus on resumes, job hunting, and presentations. These are core functions of any career, and embedding AI into your process should feel natural. There is a bonus chapter on AI stock picking.

The chapters on AI in Daily Life talk about the use of AI in the operating room, on the high seas, behind the wheel of a car, in the air, and on the battlefield. These chapters give you a glimpse of the current state of AI and where it is headed in each industry.

The future is already here, and it is not evenly distributed. This book is an attempt to distribute it a little more fairly.

I. GETTING STARTED

Any sufficiently advanced technology is indistinguishable from magic.

~Arthur C. Clarke, science-fiction novelist.

The question I often hear is, "How do I get started with AI?" Most of the time, the person asking has a creeping sense of FOMO, which in this case, is a positive force.

This section of the book will banish your FOMO and provide a practical approach to understanding and using AI. If our goal is No Adult Left Behind, we have to make sure you know how to start.

1. Search/Chatbot/Agent

When most people say they are "using AI," they mean one of three different things. They might be searching on Google. They might be having a conversation with Claude. Or they might be running an autonomous agent that is out in the world doing things on their behalf while they drink coffee.

These three experiences feel superficially similar because they all involve typing a question into a box and getting something useful back. But they are as different from each other as a library card, a research assistant, and a personal chief of staff.

Getting this distinction changes how you use these tools, what you trust them to do, and how much time you save or waste depending on whether you reached for the right one. So let's look at each one carefully.

Search: The world's biggest index card

Google Search is not artificial intelligence in the way most people think of it. It is, at its core, a sophisticated indexing system. Twenty-four hours a day, seven days a week, Google's computers are crawling the web. Every time a new page goes up anywhere in the world, Google's software finds it, reads it, identifies the keywords and topics on the page, and files that information away in an enormous index on Google's servers. When you type "best Italian restaurant in Nashville" into the search bar, Google does not go out and find Italian restaurants in Nashville in that moment. It checks its index for pages that were previously tagged as being about Italian restaurants in Nashville, and it returns a ranked list of links to those pages.

Google Search does not store the website. It stores a pointer to the website. The distinction matters.

Think of it like the card catalog at an old-fashioned library. The card catalog does not contain the books. It contains information about where the books are. When you look up a title, the catalog tells you that the book exists and gives you the shelf number. You still have to go find the book yourself.

Search is brilliant for certain things. If you want to find a specific page that exists somewhere on the internet, or if you need to navigate to a business website, check a news article, look up a definition, or find the phone number of a plumber in your zip code, search is fast and reliable. It has become smarter over the years, incorporating some AI features that can surface direct answers at the top of the page without requiring you to click through anywhere.

But at its foundation, search is a retrieval and routing tool. It finds things and points you at them. It does not think, synthesize, or converse.

The limitation of search becomes obvious the moment your question gets even slightly complicated. If you type "how do I negotiate a better deal on a car lease," Google will return a list of articles that might be helpful. You will need to click on several, read through them, sort out the good advice from the bad, figure out which parts apply to your situation, and piece together your own answer. Google will not do that for you. That is where chatbots come in.

Chatbots: The knowledgeable librarian

One of the AI engines I use gave me a comparison that I have not found a better way to improve on: "Think of a chatbot as a knowledgeable librarian you can talk to, while an AI agent is a capable intern you can delegate work to."

A chatbot is a conversational AI system. The major ones you have likely heard of are ChatGPT (from OpenAI), Claude (from Anthropic), Gemini (from Google), Copilot (from Microsoft) and Grok (from X). These systems were trained on enormous quantities of text and images including books, articles, websites, academic papers, code, and just about everything else that has been written down and is accessible. Through that training, they developed the ability to understand language, reason about questions, and generate coherent, relevant responses.

When you ask a chatbot a question, it draws on what it learned during training and tailors the answer to your question. (It only searches the internet when you ask it to, or when it has a tool enabled.) The experience is nothing like search. It is closer to talking with a well-read friend who has a lot of patience.

Here is a practical example of where a chatbot beats search cold. Say you are preparing for a performance review, and you want to ask your manager for a significant raise. You could Google "how to ask for a raise" and read through ten different articles with generic advice.

Or you could open a chatbot and explain your actual situation: you have been at the company for three years, you recently took on a major new responsibility, the industry benchmark for your role is about fifteen percent above what you are currently making, and your manager responds well to data rather than emotion. The chatbot will give you advice that accounts for all those specifics. It will suggest the language to use, anticipate the objections your manager might raise, and help you prepare a response to each one. It is a conversation, not a retrieval of data.

Chatbots are also excellent when the information you need is contained within a specific set of documents rather than across the entire internet. Many companies now deploy chatbots on top of their own internal materials, things like technical manuals, employee handbooks, product catalogs, and customer service databases.

A customer service chatbot for an appliance company does not need access to the whole web. It needs to know everything in that company's documentation and inventory. You ask it what replacement filter fits your refrigerator model, and it pulls that answer out of the product documentation instantly. You ask it what the return policy is on open-box items, and it tells you without requiring you to read the entire terms of service. That is a chatbot doing what a chatbot is designed to do.

Amazon has a chatbot called Rufus embedded in its shopping app. You may have encountered it. It is that awkward little assistant in the corner that asks if you need help to find something. Rufus is trained on Amazon's product catalog and customer reviews. You can ask it questions like "What is the difference between an air fryer and a convection oven?" and it will give you a reasonable answer based on product descriptions and customer feedback. It is not the most sophisticated AI you will ever use, but it illustrates the principle well. The chatbot does not know everything about the world. It knows what it was trained on, and within that domain, it is fast and useful.

The major limitation of a chatbot is that it requires you to drive. It answers questions and follows instructions, but it waits for each one. It is good at giving you information, analysis, and recommendations, but is not designed to go out and take action in the world on your behalf. For that, you need an agent.

Agents: The capable intern

An AI agent is a different animal. Where a chatbot responds to your prompts, an agent acts on your behalf. Where a chatbot synthesizes information, an agent executes tasks. And where a chatbot simply answers your next question, an agent can plan a sequence of steps, make decisions along the way, and complete a goal with minimal supervision from you.

The travel planning example is a useful one because almost everyone has experienced how tedious the process is without help. Planning a long weekend trip requires you to check your calendar, search flights on one or two airline sites, compare prices, book a seat, navigate to a car rental site, check availability, pick a car, enter your details, confirm the reservation, find a hotel near where you need to be, read the reviews, check for available dates, book the room, and then somehow coordinate all of those confirmations so that everything lines up. If you have done this recently, you know it takes the better part of an evening.

A properly designed agent can do all of that for you. But before it can, you have to do something important: set it up correctly.

This is where a lot of people get into trouble with agents, so pay attention. Go to ChatGPT and set up a Custom GPT or use Claude Cowork, which is a super-agent, to set up the task you want the agent to handle.

Before you hand an agent any responsibility, you need to have a careful conversation about permissions and preferences. What is the agent allowed to do? What is it not allowed to do? Where does it have the authority to make a commitment on your behalf, and where does it need to stop and ask you first?

For the "travel agent," start with your calendar. You give the agent read access, so it knows when you are free and you can decide whether the agent can also write to your calendar or whether it must ask you before scheduling anything. Then you connect the agent to your airline frequent flyer account and set your preferences: window seat, no red-eye flights, and a specific airline if you have one. You connect it to your car rental account and tell it you prefer a mid-size sedan or something with better gas mileage. You connect it to your hotel account and specify that you want to stay within a reasonable distance of the city center, that you prefer a property with a gym, and that a checkout time before eleven o'clock is a deal-breaker.

With all of that in place, you tell the agent: "I need to get to Chicago the first weekend in May, arriving Friday afternoon and returning Sunday evening. Find me flights, a car, and a hotel and bring me back the options before booking anything."

The agent goes to work. It checks your calendar, confirms the weekend is free, searches flights, narrows the results based on your preferences, checks car availability, cross-references hotel options against your criteria, and comes back with a summary for your approval. You review it, make any changes, and authorize the bookings. The agent handles the rest.

That is the best version of how this works. The cautionary version, if you will, is the agent that was given too much authority too early. Take the same scenario, but this time tell the agent to "Just book everything." You come back an hour later to find you are committed to a non-refundable hotel in a neighborhood you do not recognize, a rental car upgrade you did not need, and a connecting flight through a city that adds three hours to your trip because a non-stop option was five dollars more expensive.

Agents are powerful tools, but power without supervision is exactly as dangerous as it sounds.

The principle here is simple enough. Start narrow. Give the agent a clearly bounded task. Review what it did before letting it do more. As you build trust with a particular agent and understand how it makes decisions, you can expand its authority. Treat it the way you would treat a new employee who is capable and enthusiastic but still learning your preferences. You would not give a new hire the company credit card and full signing authority on the first day. The same logic applies.

Beyond travel, agents are starting to appear in other areas of everyday professional life. A research agent can be given a list of competitors and asked to monitor their websites, press releases, and job postings, then deliver a weekly summary of anything significant that has changed. A sales agent can be connected to a CRM, given a list of target accounts, and tasked with drafting personalized outreach emails based on each prospect's recent activity. A scheduling agent can manage your calendar, handle meeting requests, and protect certain blocks of time without requiring you to be involved in every exchange.

None of these things are science fiction. They are available now, many of them on platforms that do not require any programming knowledge.

Knowing which tool to grab

Since the goal of this chapter is not just to explain these tools but to make you more effective at using them, here are my recommendations.

Reach for search when you need to find something that exists somewhere on the internet and you need to be pointed toward it. A news article, a product page, a government form, a phone number, or a restaurant address. Search is fast, reliable, and requires no prompting skill.

Reach for a chatbot when you need to think through something, get personalized advice, have a document explained or edited, prepare for a presentation, or brainstorm ideas. Chatbots reward good questions. The more context you give them about your situation, the better the answer you get back.

Reach for an agent when you have a repeating task with clear steps that currently costs you significant time, and when you are willing to invest the upfront work of setting it up correctly. Agents are not for one-time tasks. They earn their keep through repetition.

The most important thing to understand is that these three tools are not competing with each other. They are different instruments. A carpenter does not debate whether to use a hammer or a saw. The question is what you are trying to build to be useful in your daily life.

2. User Manuals

Nobody reads the manual. Let's just get that on the table.

You buy a new appliance, a piece of electronics, a piece of exercise equipment, or a home security system, whatever it is, and somewhere in the box is a booklet. Maybe it is a thin pamphlet or a spiral-bound monument to corporate liability, printed in seven languages with diagrams that appear to have been drawn by someone who has never seen the product. You look at it briefly, set it aside, and try to figure the thing out by pressing buttons until something happens.

This is a rational response to user manuals, which are almost universally terrible. They are written by engineers for engineers. They assume you care about every feature rather than just the three you will use. They are organized by component rather than by task, which means the answer to "why isn't this working" requires you to know which component to blame before you can find the relevant section. They use terminology that is specific to the product and never defined, and they make you feel stupid for needing them in the first place.

The result is that most people either push through on their own and leave features permanently off, or they end up searching YouTube for a tutorial, or they call a family member who knows the product, or they just live with the problem.

There is now a better option, and it takes about thirty seconds.

The stereo story

The introduction to this book opened with a scene that I want to return to here because it is the cleanest illustration of what this chapter is about.

I was at a friend's house helping him install new stereo and audio equipment. We had been at it for the better part of an hour. Cables were plugged in, settings were adjusted, and nothing was working the way it should. My friend was getting frustrated. There was a manual somewhere in the pile of packaging, but neither of us had any interest in reading it.

So, I picked up my phone, took a picture of the back panel of the receiver, where all the inputs and outputs live, and uploaded it to ChatGPT. I described the problem we were having: the speakers were connected, but the sound was coming out muffled, or not at all, and we could not figure out why. I asked the AI to troubleshoot the issue based on what it could see in the photo and what I had described.

In a few seconds, it came back with four specific things to check, listed in order of likelihood. The second one fixed the problem. Total time from photo to working audio system: about three minutes.

My friend, who is smart and capable, was staggered. Not by the technology exactly, but by the casualness of the whole thing. I had not announced that I was going to use AI. I had not made a show of it. I had done it the way you reach for your phone to look something up: automatically, without drama, because it was the obvious next move.

That is the mindset shift this chapter is asking you to make. When something is not working and you do not know why, your first move should be to show the AI the problem and ask for help. Not a YouTube video or a call to customer service where you will be on hold for the rest of your life and then speak with someone reading from the same manual you ignored. Take a picture. Ask the question. Get the answer.

What the AI can see

The reason this works so well is that modern AI systems are good at interpreting images, especially images of physical objects with text, labels, ports, buttons, and indicators on them. The back of an audio receiver is a good example. There are inputs and outputs for different signal types. There are labels in small print. There are color-coded ports that correspond to a wiring scheme that you are supposed to know already. When a human looks at it and does not know audio equipment, it is a wall of confusing hardware. When an AI looks at it, it recognizes the component type, identifies the ports, understands the signal flow, and can reason about what a given configuration of cables means for how the system will or will not work.

The same capability applies across a range of everyday situations. A circuit breaker panel where you cannot figure out which breaker controls which part of the house. The settings menu on a camera you just bought. The wiring diagram behind a thermostat you are trying to replace. The error codes on a washing machine display. The configuration page of a router that you have been staring at for twenty minutes without making progress.

In all these cases, a photograph sends the AI more useful information than almost anything you could type. You are not trying to describe a complex visual situation in words. You are showing it directly, and the AI can work with what it sees.

Upload the manual

Taking a picture is the fastest approach to a specific, immediate problem. But if you are dealing with a complex product that you plan to use regularly, there is an even more powerful option: find the manual in PDF form and upload the whole thing to the AI.

Most manufacturers now post their manuals online. Search for the product name plus "owner's manual PDF" and you will almost always find it. Download it, open your AI tool of choice, upload the document, and now you have something remarkable: a knowledgeable assistant who has read every word of that manual and is ready to answer any question you have about the product in plain English, immediately, without you having to read a single page.

This is not a small thing. Think about what it means for the kinds of products people buy and then never fully figure out.

The new treadmill that has twelve different workout programs you have never used because you could not be bothered to work through the setup. Ask the AI to walk you through configuring a thirty-minute interval training session for someone at your fitness level. Done.

The home theater receiver with HDMI switching, zone outputs, and a calibration system that came with a ninety-page manual and a calibration microphone you have never used. Upload the manual, ask the AI to walk you through the calibration process step by step, and get the sound your system can produce instead of the default settings you have been living with.

The multifunction copier in the office that everyone knows how to use for basic copying, but nobody has ever set up for double-sided scanning to email, even though that feature has been sitting there for three years. Upload the manual. Ask how. Configure it this afternoon.

The AI does not get impatient when you ask follow-up questions. It does not sigh when you need the same step explained a different way and does not have nineteen other things it needs to do. The AI has read the manual and is happy to translate it for you.

Other documents

The user manual use case extends well beyond product documentation, and this is worth slowing down on because it is where some of the most useful applications live.

Insurance policies are dense. They use defined terms that mean something specific in the insurance context and something slightly different in ordinary English, and they are intentionally written in a way that requires a trained professional to interpret fully. Most people do not know what their health insurance, homeowner's policy, or business liability coverage covers until they file a claim and discover the answer the hard way.

Upload your insurance policy to an AI and ask it specific questions. "Does this policy cover water damage from a pipe that burst inside the walls?" "What is my out-of-pocket maximum and how does it interact with my deductible?" "If I work from home and a client is injured on my property, am I covered under this homeowner's policy?"

These are questions a lawyer or insurance broker would charge you to answer. The AI will answer them in a few seconds, in plain language, with references to the specific sections of the policy that apply. The AI helps you understand a document you already own.

The same principle applies to lease agreements, mortgage documents, employee handbooks, contractor agreements, and the terms of service for software products your company relies on. Any time you have a long, complex document that you are supposed to understand but probably have not read, the AI can serve as your translator.

Take your lease agreement. Hand it to the AI and ask: "What are my obligations for repairs and maintenance? What are the conditions under which my landlord can enter the property? What happens to my security deposit if I need to break the lease early?" If you are signing a new lease, ask the AI to flag any clauses that are unusual or that would be worth negotiating before you sign. Most people sign these documents without reading them and spend years subject to terms they did not know existed.

You paid for the policy, or you signed the lease. Understanding the documents is the least you should do.

Medicine and prescription labels

Here is one that hits closer to home for a lot of people, particularly those managing medications for themselves or for aging parents. Prescription labels are written to contain the legally required information in the smallest possible space. They are not written to be understood. "Take one tablet by mouth twice daily with or without food. Avoid prolonged exposure to sunlight. Do not take with grapefruit juice. Contact physician if symptoms persist." Fine.

But what happens when you are taking four medications and you cannot remember which one conflicts with which food, or whether the interaction warning you read somewhere applies to your specific combination?

Photograph the label. Ask the AI to explain what the instructions mean in practical terms and flag anything you should watch for. If you have multiple prescriptions, you can photograph all the labels and ask the AI whether there are any known interactions between them that you should be aware of. This is not a substitute for talking to your pharmacist or doctor. It is a way to walk into that conversation with better questions.

For those managing elderly relatives, this application is significant. Medication regimens for older patients can be complex, involving a dozen or more prescriptions with different timing requirements, food interactions, and side effects to monitor. The AI will not replace the physician, but it can help a family member understand what they are managing and what questions to ask.

Product recalls and safety notices work in the same way. If you receive a recall notice for an appliance and the instructions for what to do are written in the style of a government document, which is to say, not for human beings, photograph it and ask the AI to tell you in two sentences what you are supposed to do.

A few things to keep in mind

This chapter would not be complete without a note on where the approach has limits. The AI is working with what you show it. If the photo is blurry, poorly lit, or cuts off part of the panel or label, the AI will do its best, but it may miss something or misread a label. Take a clear photo. It takes an extra five seconds, and it matters.

For safety-critical applications, treat the AI's answer as a starting point, not a final authority. Electrical work, gas appliances, structural modifications, and anything medical should always involve a qualified professional in the loop. The AI can help you understand what you are looking at and ask better questions, but there is no substitute for a licensed electrician when the stakes involve fire or electrocution.

The AI can misread a label or misidentify a component, particularly on older or less common products where its training data may be thinner. This is the "edge case" we mention throughout this book. If the answer it gives you does not match what you see in front of you, push back. Describe what you are observing and ask it to reconsider.

Finally, if you upload a document to an AI tool and that document contains sensitive personal or financial information, pay attention to the privacy settings of the platform you are using. Most major AI tools have settings that allow you to limit how your data is used. For documents that contain your financial records, medical history, or personal identifying information, it is worth spending two minutes understanding the privacy policy of the tool before you upload.

The bigger point

The stereo story that opened this book was not a demonstration of exotic technology. It was a demonstration of a habit. The habit of reaching for AI when something is confusing rather than either struggling through it alone or giving up. That habit, once developed, becomes automatic, and it saves real time and real frustration daily.

Forget the manual and take a picture.

3. Prompts

Everything we cover in this book, the resume help, the interview prep, the stock research, and the presentation drafts, all of it depends on one skill that most people never bother to develop. It is the single biggest factor separating the people who get something useful out of AI from those who try it twice, conclude it is overrated, and go back to Googling things.

That skill is prompting.

A prompt is simply what you type into the AI. It is the instruction or the question. It sounds trivial until you realize that the same AI engine, given two different prompts on the same topic, can produce output that ranges from spectacularly awesome to completely useless.

The old programming adage applies here more than almost anywhere else: "garbage in, garbage out." The machine will do its best with whatever you hand it. If you hand it a vague, lazy, context-free question, it will give you a vague, lazy, context-free answer. If you hand it a well-constructed prompt that explains your situation, your goal, your constraints, and your audience, it will give you something worth reading.

Learning to write good prompts is the highest-return investment you can make as an AI user. It costs nothing, takes a few hours of practice, and will immediately improve every interaction you have with any AI tool.

The most common mistake

Type "should I lease or buy a car" into Google and you will get a reasonable list of articles covering the general topic. That works fine for a general question.

Type the exact same thing into Gemini or Grok and you will get a reasonable general answer about the pros and cons of leasing versus buying. It will cover interest rates, depreciation, mileage limits, flexibility, and the typical decision framework. Accurate. Helpful in the way that a Wikipedia article is helpful.

What it will not do is tell you what to do. Because it does not know who you are.

That is the mistake. People use AI the same way they use search, as a retrieval tool that they point at a question and expect to return a useful result. Search rewards brevity. A shorter, well-chosen search query often returns better results than a long, rambling one. People carry that habit into AI, and it produces mediocre outcomes.

AI rewards the opposite. With AI, more context is more. Much more.

Here is the prompt I used when I was working through the buy-versus-lease question for a car. "I have a salary of $125,000 per year and $50,000 in savings. I am looking at cars that cost about $45,000. Is it better for me to lease or purchase the car?" That prompt gave the AI something real to work with. My income, my savings, and the price range I was considering. With that information, the AI could reason about what a $9,000 down payment would mean relative to my total savings, what monthly payment levels were appropriate for my income, and whether my remaining cash on hand after a purchase would leave me financially comfortable or dangerously exposed.

The AI asked follow-up questions. Did I plan to keep the car for several years, or did I want a new model every few years? Did I have stable employment, or was there a reasonable scenario where my income could change? Those questions came because the AI was treating the conversation like a real consultation, which is exactly what you want. And that conversation only started because the initial prompt gave it enough to work with.

Think of it this way. When you call a doctor with a medical question, the doctor does not just answer the question you asked. She asks you questions. How long has this been happening? Where exactly does it hurt? Do you have any other symptoms? She is gathering context before she gives you advice, because advice without context is just guessing.

AI works the same way, and a good prompt front-loads the context so the AI can skip the twenty questions and get straight to something useful.

The professor analogy

The best mental model for prompting an AI is to imagine you are asking a question of a knowledgeable college professor who has no idea who you are or what your situation is.

The professor knows a lot about almost every subject. She has read more on the topic than you will ever read. She is interested in helping you think through your problem. But she is meeting you for the first time, and she needs you to brief her on your situation before she can give you advice that is relevant to your life rather than to the general case.

If you walk into her office and say, "Should I change careers?" She will give you a thoughtful but generic answer about factors to consider when changing careers. If you sit down and tell her that you have been in financial services for eighteen years, you recently ran a P&L for a mid-size division, you are increasingly interested in the nonprofit sector, your youngest child starts college in two years which creates a financial constraint, and you have a specific organization in mind that you have been watching for some time, she will give you advice you can use.

It's the same professor, but the answers differ because the second version of you was willing to brief her properly. The professor does not judge you for the length of the briefing. She does not get impatient when you give her more detail. She is there for the consultation. Use the time.

Four things for a good prompt

There is no magic formula, but good prompts usually share four elements, and keeping these in mind will improve almost any request you make.

The first is context. Who are you, what is your situation, and why does this question matter? The AI does not know you are a mid-career professional in a regulated industry with a risk-averse board and a team that has never worked with AI before. Tell it. That information changes the answer significantly.

The second is the specific task. Tell the AI what you want as the actual deliverable. "Help me think through my marketing strategy" is a topic. "Write a two-paragraph summary of our Q3 marketing performance that I can paste into the board deck, written for a board audience that cares about revenue contribution and cost efficiency" is a task. The second version gives the AI a specific thing to produce, which is far more useful.

The third is format. Do you want bullet points or paragraphs? A list of options or a single recommendation? A short answer or a detailed analysis? A table comparing three alternatives? The AI is flexible on format, but it will default to something generic if you do not specify. Tell it what you want the output to look like.

The fourth is constraints. What should the AI avoid? How long should the answer be? Are there topics that are off-limits or considerations that must be included? Constraints help the AI narrow its focus instead of producing something comprehensive that covers every angle when you only needed one.

A prompt that addresses all four does not have to be long. It just must be specific. Here is an example of a weak prompt and a stronger version of the same request.

Weak: "Write a cover letter for a marketing job."

Stronger: "Write a cover letter for a Director of Marketing position at a mid-size consumer goods company. I have twelve years of experience in brand management, most recently leading a team of eight at a company with $200 million in revenue. The job description emphasizes digital marketing and data-driven decision-making, which I want to address directly. The tone should be confident but not boastful. Keep it to three paragraphs and under 300 words."

The second prompt will produce something you can send. The first will produce something you have to rewrite completely, which defeats the purpose.

Give the AI a role

One of the most effective prompting techniques is to assign the AI a specific role before you ask your question.

"What should I consider before accepting a job offer?" is a reasonable question that will get a reasonable answer. "You are an executive coach with twenty years of experience advising senior professionals on career transitions. What should I consider before accepting a job offer that comes with a significant title change but a lateral compensation move?" is the same question framed from a specific perspective, and it will produce a more targeted and useful response.

The role framing works because AI systems are trained on huge amounts of text from many contexts, perspectives, and levels of expertise. When you specify a role, you are helping the AI weight its response toward the knowledge base that is most relevant to your situation.

An executive coach thinks about career transitions differently than a general career advisor, who thinks about it differently than a compensation specialist, who thinks about it differently than a recruiter. Same question, different lenses, and meaningfully different answers.

You can also assign the AI a role that represents your audience rather than an advisor. "Read this proposal as a skeptical CFO and tell me what objections you would raise" is a powerful editorial tool. So is "review this email as if you are the person receiving it and tell me what your first reaction is."

Prompting is a conversation

Most people treat AI like a vending machine. Put in a question, get out an answer, move on. That is the least effective way to use it.

The AI remembers the entire conversation you are having with it, and every follow-up question builds on what came before. This means you can start with a rough prompt, see what comes back, and then refine from there. "Make that shorter." "Focus more on the financial risks and less on the operational side." "Now rewrite it for an audience that is skeptical of this idea." "Give me three versions of the opening paragraph, and let me choose."

This iterative approach is how the AI becomes useful. The first response is rarely the final product. It is the beginning of a conversation that narrows toward what you need. Professional writers who use AI regularly describe the process as collaborative drafting: the AI produces material rapidly and at scale; the human shapes, redirects, and refines. Neither one alone would produce the same result. This is the future of writing.

Do not be shy about pushing back. If the AI gives you something generic, tell it. "This is too generic. I need something more specific to my industry and my specific challenge. Try again with the additional context that my company has been losing market share to newer competitors who are selling directly to consumers, while we still rely on retail distribution." The AI will not be offended. It will not sulk. It will try again with the new information, and the second attempt will almost always be better.

The multi-step trick

One of the more powerful techniques to emerge from experimenting with AI is using multiple AI interactions in sequence, where the output of one becomes the input for the next.

The interview preparation process from an earlier chapter is a good illustration. In step one, you ask an AI to predict the interview questions for a specific role and suggest strong answers. In step two, you take those answers and feed them to a different AI system, asking it to evaluate them as a hiring manager would. In step three, you ask another AI to assess whether the answers sound coached or authentic. Each step builds on the last, and the final product is more rigorously tested than anything a single prompt could produce. Try this, it is pretty cool.

The same logic applies to any high-stakes document. Draft a proposal with one AI session, then open a fresh session and ask the AI to play a skeptical reader and identify the weakest arguments. Open another session and ask the AI to check the document for any claims that would need verification before you could stand behind them in a room full of experts.

Each pass is a different lens, and together they approximate the kind of review you would get from a team of colleagues if you had the time and access.

This is not as complicated as it sounds. It is simply the discipline of not accepting the first response as the final answer.

The mistakes that will cost time

Three prompting habits reliably produce bad outcomes, and they are worth naming directly. Being vague on purpose because you are not sure what you want. This produces an answer that forces you to clarify what you wanted, which means you are essentially writing the real prompt in round two anyway. Think through what you want before you type. Even sixty seconds of thinking before opening the AI will improve the result. (Some would say that this advice applies to any time you speak.)

Asking multiple unrelated questions in a single prompt. The AI will answer all of them, but not well, because it is splitting its focus across things that have nothing to do with each other. Ask one thing at a time and finish that conversation before starting a new one.

Accepting the first response when it is not quite right and then complaining that AI does not work is like going to a restaurant, ordering steak, receiving something that is not cooked the way you wanted it, and leaving without saying anything to the waiter. Say something. Tell the AI what it got wrong and ask it to try again. The correction is almost always fast, and the result is almost always better.

The last thing

People ask me sometimes how long a prompt should be. There is no limit. None. I have seen prompts that run for several pages of text, where someone pasted in an entire document and asked the AI to do something specific with it. Those prompts work fine.

The prompt should be as long as it needs to be to give the AI the context it needs to do the job well. You are not being graded on brevity. Give the AI what it needs.

The best way to get better at prompting is to do it more and pay attention to what changes when you change your prompts. You will develop an instinct for it faster than you expect, and once you have it, every AI tool you use gets more useful overnight.

II. AI AND CAREERS

AI... if you don't understand it, learn it. Because otherwise, you're going to be a dinosaur within three years.

~Mark Cuban, Entrepreneur

Now that you understand the basics of AI: you know when to use AI vs search, you know how to write a prompt, and other basic skills, let's cut to the chase.

How can AI help me find a job, change careers, or excel at my current job? This section of the book will give you the roadmap of the must-have AI skills in today's professional world.

Let's face the fact that if everyone else is using AI to advance themselves and you are not, you could be left behind.

4. Getting Hired

You have spent three hours finding a job posting that excites you. "Senior consultant," at a company you respect, and a role that fits your background. You tweak your resume, write a cover letter, upload everything to the employer's portal, and wait. A week passes. Then two. You get a form email telling you that the position has been filled. You never spoke to a human being.

What happened in that portal is worth understanding because it is happening to millions of people right now, and most of them have no idea how the game is being played.

The machine is reading your resume before any human does.

When you apply to a mid-size or large employer today, there is a good chance that the first reviewer of your resume is not a person. It is an AI screening tool. The hiring manager has a stack of three hundred applications and needs to get to a manageable shortlist. Rather than read every resume, the AI does an initial pass. It scans for keywords that match the job description: specific degrees, years of experience, job titles, technical skills, and industry terminology. It checks for signals of cultural or stylistic fit based on your social-media presence, how you write and present yourself, and compares your profile against patterns from previous successful hires.

If your resume does not speak the language the AI is looking for, it does not matter how qualified you are. You never get to the human.

This is frustrating, and I will say more about the problems it creates later in this chapter. But right now, let's talk about what you can do about it.

The answer is to use the same tool that they are using. If the employer is deploying AI to screen candidates, there is no reason you should submit a resume you wrote entirely on your own with no AI assistance. That is like showing up to a Formula One race in a compact car.

Building a resume that gets through

Start with your resume as it currently exists. It does not need to be perfect. Open Claude, ChatGPT, or the AI of your choice, paste in the resume, and paste in the job description you are applying for. Then ask the AI something like this: "Here is my resume and here is the job description I am applying for. Rewrite my resume so that it is tailored to this specific role, using language and keywords from the job description wherever my experience supports it. Keep everything accurate and do not invent experience I do not have."

That last instruction matters. You are not asking the AI to fabricate anything. You are asking it to present what you have done in the language that the employer's screening tool is looking for. The experience is real. The translation is what the AI provides.

What comes back will typically be a tighter, sharper version of what you submitted. The AI will have reorganized your bullet points so that the most relevant experience comes first. It will have swapped out your generic language for the specific terminology the employer used in the posting. If the job description says "cross-functional stakeholder management" and your resume says, "worked with different departments," the AI will update the language to match while still describing the same actual work you did.

Do this for every application. It sounds like more work than it is. Once you have a strong base resume, each tailored version takes about ten minutes. The people who are getting interviews right now are the people who are doing this. The people submitting the same resume to every posting are the ones getting the form rejection emails.

A few practical notes. Read the AI's output carefully before you submit it. The AI does not know your career the way you do, and occasionally it will phrase something in a way that is technically accurate but not quite how you would describe yourself. Fix those before you send anything. Your voice still matters. You also want to make sure the resume is honest. The AI is a translator and an editor, but you own the final product.

One more thing about resumes. Once you have a polished version, feed it back to the AI and ask it to play the role of a screening algorithm. "Imagine you are an AI hiring tool reviewing this resume for the following job description. What would you flag as strong matches? What gaps or weaknesses would you identify?" This gives you a view from the other side of the process, and it will often surface things you would not have thought to fix on your own.

The credentials vs. capabilities shift

Before we get to interview preparation, it is worth stepping back and understanding something that has changed in the job market over the last decade because it affects how you position yourself at every stage of the process.

There was a time when the name of your college on a resume opened doors almost automatically.

Companies would send recruiters directly to the campuses of elite universities and fight for access to those students. A degree from a well-regarded institution, regardless of what you studied, was essentially a floor pass that guaranteed you at least a conversation. That era is over.

The AI engines I queried on this topic were pretty blunt about it: there has been a distinct shift from credentials to capabilities. Everybody has credentials now. Grade inflation has made the competition almost meaningless. At Ivy League schools, sixty to seventy percent of all grades are A's. The average unweighted GPA for college-educated applicants is hovering around 3.7 or 3.8. If everybody is above average, then average means nothing.

What employers are looking for now is evidence that you can do something. They want to see what you studied, not just where. Internships, real work experience, projects, and problems you've solved need to be highlighted. They want capabilities, and capabilities come from doing things, not from a brand name on the diploma.

This should encourage many people. If you did not go to a prestigious school but have spent years developing real skills and solving real problems, the playing field has shifted in your favor in ways it did not twenty years ago. The kid who skipped the four-year university and spent twelve weeks in a Python coding bootcamp is getting hired to build AI tools while people with sparkling GPAs are still tweaking their resumes. That is not an exaggeration. That is the market right now.

The practical implication for your job search is this: your resume and your interview answers need to lead with what you have done and what you can do, not with where you studied or what your title was. AI can help you make that shift in framing, but you need to give it the raw material to shape.

Using AI to prepare for an interview

Let's assume the resume worked and you have an interview scheduled. This is where AI preparation gets powerful, and where a lot of candidates are leaving opportunity on the table by not using it.

The basic approach is straightforward. Take the job description and feed it to two or three different AI systems. Ask each one the same question: "Based on this job description, what questions is this interviewer most likely to ask, and what would a strong answer to each question look like?" You will get slightly different lists from different AI engines, which is useful. Take the combined output, and you will have a comprehensive map of what is coming.

Now do a second pass. Take those AI-generated sample answers and feed them to a different AI system, this time asking it to play the role of a skeptical hiring manager. "Here are sample answers to common interview questions for this role. If you were the hiring manager, what would you push back on? What would make you doubt the candidate? What follow-up questions would you ask?" This is the part most people skip, and it is the part with the biggest pay off. The AI will poke holes in the generic answers in the same way an experienced interviewer would, and you will be better prepared for the live conversation as a result.

Most roles at the professional level also require behavioral interview questions, which usually follow the STAR method. STAR stands for Situation, Task, Action, Result. The interviewer asks you to tell them about a time you dealt with a difficult client, or led a team through a crisis, or made a mistake and had to recover from it. The expectation is that your answer follows a structured arc: here is the situation, here is what I was responsible for, here is what I did, and here is what happened as a result.

AI is good at helping you prepare STAR answers because STAR answers require a kind of structured storytelling that most people find unnatural under pressure. Take three or four experiences from your career that you are proud of or that involved difficulty. Describe each one to the AI in rough terms. Then ask it to help you shape each story into a clean STAR narrative that is concise, honest, and emphasizes the key point. Practice reading those out loud. The goal is not to memorize a script. The goal is to internalize the structure so that when you are sitting across from an interviewer and they ask you about a situation when you dealt with a difficult team member, you can reach for the right story and tell it well.

There is one more AI preparation technique worth mentioning, and it requires a little courage. At the end of your preparation session, ask the AI to conduct a full mock interview with you in real time. Tell it to play the role of a hiring manager for the specific role you are applying for and not to go easy on you.

Type your answers as you would say them out loud. When you finish, ask the AI for honest feedback: what came across well, what sounded rehearsed, what was vague, and what you should strengthen. If you can get through one or two of these mock sessions before the real thing, you will walk into the interview with an improved level of confidence.

The battle of the bots

If AI is helping you prepare near-perfect answers to interview questions, and it is also helping thousands of other candidates do the same thing, then the interview signal that hiring managers thought they were reading has changed. The natural fluency, the quick thinking, the self-awareness that used to distinguish a strong candidate from an average one is now a skill that can be rehearsed to near-perfection overnight with the right AI prompts. (This is no different from the booming industry of standardized test preparation.)

An average candidate who prepares thoroughly with AI can walk into an interview and sound just as polished as someone who is naturally exceptional. That is not a good thing, for the exceptional candidates or for the hiring managers who are trying to find them.

The hiring managers who are still relying on AI-filtered resumes and a single structured interview are going to notice that all their finalists sound the same. Every answer is crisp and structured. Every story has a clear beginning, middle, and end. Everybody handled that difficult situation with grace and came out the other side with a lesson learned. It is beginning to look a lot like every candidate attended the same coaching seminar, because in a sense they did, and the coach was one of the AIs.

This is not a reason to avoid AI preparation. It is a reason to go further than AI preparation. The companies and hiring managers who figure this out first will start putting more weight on the things AI cannot replicate: the unscripted conversation, the follow-up question that catches you off guard, the instinct that comes through when somebody has lived the experience they are describing versus when they rehearsed a convincing version of it.

Some companies are already moving back toward more in-person time earlier in the process, specifically because the virtual, asynchronous, AI-managed hiring funnel has stopped being a useful signal.

As a candidate, the lesson is that AI can help you prepare to get in the game, but you still have to win on your own.

The thing AI cannot replicate

I have spoken with many people over the years who were in job searches and feeling beaten up by the process. The machine-driven application system is flat-out demoralizing. You put real effort into an application, you hear nothing back, and you have no idea whether any human being ever looked at what you submitted. The feedback loop is essentially broken.

My advice to people in that situation has always been the same, and AI has not changed it: get out and talk to people.

I once worked at a company that grew from a startup to over three thousand employees, and for most of that journey, every new hire had to know somebody at the company. Not a close friend, not a family member. Just someone who could say, "I met this person and they seem sharp." That kind of warm introduction bypassed the entire screening algorithm, not because the company was a bed of nepotism, but because a human vouching for another human is a far better signal than a resume-scoring system since, in a sense, the recommender is sticking his neck out and taking a risk by recommending a new hire.

That pattern has not gone away. If anything, as the AI-driven process has become more impersonal, the human touchpoint matters more, not less. A warm introduction from a former colleague, a conversation at an industry event, a thoughtful note to someone whose work you admire, or a call with a former professor who knows someone at the company you want to join. None of these things require credentials or optimized resumes. They require initiative and the willingness to put yourself in front of real people.

AI is an extraordinary tool for preparing to be your best self in the interview. It will not get you the introduction.

Always be upskilling

One final point that applies to getting hired and staying hired in equal measure.

The job market is experiencing an oversupply problem right now. Recent data suggests that more than half of college graduates are in jobs that do not require a college degree. The competition for good positions is fierce, the screening tools are ruthless, and the economy is not generating jobs as fast as it is generating qualified candidates. In that environment, sitting still is a strategy for falling behind.

Upskilling is the word that keeps coming up when AI is asked about career success. It is not a glamorous word, but it is an accurate one. Upskilling means continuously adding capabilities to what you already know how to do. It is the same instinct that sent the earlier generation to night school to learn Excel or pushed people to figure out the internet when it was new and painfully slow. The people who added the new capability early had a real advantage over those who waited to see if it would stick.

AI fluency is the upskilling priority of this moment. Not programming and not data science. Simply knowing how to use the tools well enough that you can apply them to problems in your field, communicate about them intelligently with colleagues and employers, and continue learning as they evolve. Every chapter in this book is part of that process.

The people on the other side of the interview table know this too. When they see a candidate who has clearly been using AI as part of his workflow and can speak about it specifically and honestly, it registers. It signals adaptability, which is exactly what every hiring manager is trying to find.

Always be upskilling.

5. Stock Picking

Before we get into this chapter, a disclaimer. The information here is for general educational purposes only and does not constitute financial, investment, or legal advice. I am not a licensed financial advisor, and all investment decisions are your own responsibility. Consult a professional before making any financial decisions. You have been warned.

Now that we have that out of the way, let's talk about whether AI can pick stocks.

This is one of the most common questions I get, and I understand why. The idea is seductive. AI can read everything. It knows every earnings report, every analyst note, every news article, and every regulatory filing. It does not sleep, it does not get emotional, and it does not panic-sell because its brother-in-law told it something at Thanksgiving. If anything should be able to beat the market, shouldn't it be the machine that knows everything?

The honest answer, which this chapter will walk you through with real numbers and real results, is probably not. But the more interesting answer is that asking the question that way misses the point. AI is useful in investing, just not in the way most people expect.

The benchmark that beats everyone

Before we get to AI, let's establish the baseline that everything else should be measured against: the S&P 500.

When people say, "the market," they are almost always referring to the S&P 500, which is a basket of 500 of the largest publicly traded companies in the United States, spread across every sector of the economy. You have technology companies, banks, healthcare companies, retailers, energy companies, and consumer brands. All of them, bundled together into a single index.

You can buy the S&P 500 directly through any brokerage account by purchasing a low-cost index fund, often with a ticker symbol like SPY or VOO. When you do that, you own a tiny piece of all 500 companies simultaneously. When the index goes up, you go up. When it goes down, you go down. Boring, but effective.

Over the last twenty years, the S&P 500 has returned an average of about eleven percent per year. If you put $1,000 into an S&P 500 index fund twenty years ago and left it alone, you would have more than $8,000 today. No stock picking, no late nights reading annual reports, no watching financial television. Just patience.

Here is the number that should stop you cold before you do anything else with this chapter. Over a twenty-year period, approximately ninety percent of professional money managers, the people whose entire job is to pick stocks and beat the market, fail to outperform the S&P 500. They charge you a management fee, often two percent of your assets per year, for the privilege of underperforming an index fund you can buy for nearly free. The exceptions exist. There are managers with superior long-term track records. They are rare, they are hard to identify in advance, and the fees still eat into your returns.

So, the question of whether AI can pick stocks that beat the S&P 500 is a high bar. Nine out of ten professionals with decades of experience and entire research teams behind them cannot clear it. Let's see what happened when I put the question directly to the machines.

Experiment: AI to pick three winners

I posed the following question to ChatGPT and Claude: pick three stocks that you think will move higher, on a percentage basis, than the S&P 500 over the next four weeks. Give me the rationale for each pick.

Four weeks was a deliberate choice. I figured most of you were not interested in waiting a decade to see how things turned out, and frankly, neither was I.

ChatGPT's picks were Nvidia, Tesla, and Apple. The rationale for Nvidia was that it is the dominant player in AI hardware, and upcoming news announcements could drive the stock higher. For Tesla, ChatGPT called it a momentum play, meaning investors had been piling in and could continue doing so. For Apple, the reasoning was that when investors rotate back into technology, Apple is usually the first stock they reach for.

My reaction when I read the ChatGPT picks was that they were lazy. I know a machine cannot technically be lazy, but that is the word that came to mind. These are three of the most talked-about, most analyzed, most widely held stocks on the planet. Every professional on Wall Street has a model on Nvidia. Millions of retail investors are watching Tesla's every move.

Picking these three as your best ideas is like going to a restaurant, staring at the menu for twenty minutes, and ordering a hamburger. Nothing wrong with a hamburger, but it does not suggest deep analysis.

Claude's picks were more interesting. It chose Rhythm Pharmaceuticals, Alphabet (Google's parent company), and Norwegian Cruise Line.

For Rhythm Pharmaceuticals, Claude identified a specific catalyst: the company had an FDA drug approval decision scheduled in the upcoming weeks. If the drug were to be approved, the stock could jump sharply. Claude also noted clearly that this was a binary bet. If the drug were to be rejected, the stock would likely fall just as sharply. That kind of honesty is useful.

For Alphabet, Claude described it as the more conservative pick in the group, pointing to a large backlog of contracts converting to revenue, the growing success of the Waymo autonomous vehicle division, and the rise of its Gemini AI engine. Solid reasoning, nothing flashy.

For Norwegian Cruise Line, Claude had done something clever. It identified that a large hedge fund was attempting to take over the company, and that the battle for control could drive the stock price up regardless of Norwegian's underlying business performance. That is the kind of specific, situation-based thinking that professional stock pickers get paid to do.

I found Claude's approach more rigorous. It went looking for specific reasons a stock might move, what traders call catalysts, rather than picking household names and telling me they might go up because people like them.

Results: four weeks later

Four weeks later, I went back and checked, and the results were not pretty for anyone.

The S&P 500 was down 5.4% over the period. That was a rough four weeks by any measure. The reason was a war that had broken out in Iran, which sent global oil prices higher, rattled investor confidence, and pushed money out of stocks and into cash and safer assets. Not the market environment anyone was hoping for when we started the experiment.

ChatGPT's portfolio was down 8.0%. Three technology stocks with no diversification across sectors or geographies, all hit by the same "risk-off" sentiment that pushes investors out of growth stocks when things get uncertain. The momentum strategy that might work in a calm bull market got punished in a crisis.

Claude's portfolio was down 12.4%. Ouch. Norwegian Cruise Line was crushed because an outbreak of war is just about the worst thing that can happen to a vacation company. Rhythm

Pharmaceuticals did receive its FDA approval, and the stock jumped on the day of the announcement. Then it got beaten back down over the following week as investors fled anything speculative and sat on cash. Alphabet held up relatively better but still fell with the broader market.

The S&P 500 lost the least. The diversified index, the boring one, the one that owns a piece of everything, held up better than any of the individual stock picks.

There was one more data point worth noting. Dell Technologies, which neither AI picked, was up 35% over the same four weeks. Dell posted strong earnings and had a compelling story about its position in the AI infrastructure market. The market liked it. Neither machine found it.

What the results tell us

It would be easy to look at these numbers and conclude that AI cannot pick stocks, and therefore you should not waste your time trying. But I think that conclusion is too simple and misses what was interesting about the experiment.

Claude found real catalysts. The FDA approval for Rhythm was a real event that drove a real price move, as predicted. The Norwegian Cruise Line situation was also real. The hedge fund battle was real. These were not guesses based on vibes. They were identifiable, researched reasons that a specific stock might move. The problem was not the analysis. The problem was an exogenous event, a war, that overwhelmed everything and changed the risk environment entirely.

This is the thing about stock picking that professionals will tell you quietly, if you get them in the right mood: even when you are right about the company, you can still be wrong about the timing of the stock purchase.

The market is a multivariable equation with an infinite number of inputs, many of which have nothing to do with the companies you are evaluating. A war breaks out, a central bank unexpectedly raises interest rates, or a tweet from an unpredictable political figure sends a sector into a tailspin. The best analysis in the world cannot protect you from the random events that drive markets in the short term.

What AI can do well is the research work that used to be available only to professional investors with large teams. Scanning regulatory filings for upcoming FDA decisions, identifying corporate governance situations that might trigger a price move, and aggregating news across thousands of sources to spot patterns before they become widely known. Small investors sitting at home cannot do that kind of research without AI. With it, they can. That helps, even if it does not guarantee you will beat the index.

The war trade and the peace trade

A few weeks after the initial experiment, the Iran conflict gave us a different kind of investing lesson, and the AI handled it well.

During a war, investor behavior becomes predictable in specific ways. People get conservative. They pull money out of stocks and hold cash, the way my grandmother used to liquidate everything and stuff the cash under her mattress. Several large investment funds reported record redemption requests during this period, meaning investors were not just avoiding new investments but demanding their money back to park it somewhere safe.

The money that stays in the market during a conflict tends to flow into what traders call the War Trade. Oil and defense stocks. When a war restricts the global supply of oil, prices rise and so do profits of oil companies. ExxonMobil is the obvious example. When a war requires more weapons, planes, ships, and missiles, and defense contractors profit.

Lockheed Martin is the obvious example there. These stocks go up when everything else is going down.

When the war ends, or when a ceasefire is announced, the trade reverses. This is known as the "Peace Trade." The stocks that were beaten down the most by the war conditions rebound the fastest. I asked the AI engines to think through this scenario: when the Iran war ends, which stocks will be the winners?

The answer required thinking about which companies had been hurt specifically by war conditions and why. The clearest category was airlines. Jet fuel is one of the largest costs in running an airline. When oil prices rise because of a war, airline costs go up, fares go up, traveler volumes go down, and airline stocks get punished. When oil prices fall because the conflict ends, the whole equation reverses quickly. Delta was the top pick, and the logic held up.

Consumer-spending companies were the next category. Amazon, Tesla, and similar companies get hurt during wartime not because of any direct connection to the conflict, but because rising energy costs squeeze household budgets and people pull back on discretionary spending. When energy costs ease, consumer spending rebounds.

Amazon, as the world's largest retailer, benefits directly.

The AI also pointed to small-cap stocks as strong Peace Trade candidates. Smaller companies are more sensitive to energy costs than large multinationals with sophisticated hedging strategies. An index fund covering small-cap stocks, like the iShares Russell 2000 (ticker: IWM), was the recommendation. It goes down harder in bad environments because those smaller companies have less cushion and bounce back faster when conditions improve.

Here is my favorite part of this story. We had the Peace Trade post written and were getting ready to publish it my website on a Tuesday evening. That night, President Trump announced a two-week ceasefire with Iran. By Wednesday morning, the Peace Trade was already in full swing. ExxonMobil was down ten dollars. Amazon was up eight. The small-cap IWM index was up ten. The AI's analysis had been correct in real time. We just published it about a week too late. Sorry.

How to use AI for investing

So where does this leave you as someone thinking about using AI to manage investments or make better financial decisions?

The first and most important point is to understand what AI is good at in this context and what it is not. AI is not a prediction machine. The professional money managers who beat the market over time are not doing it by predicting the unpredictable. They are doing it by having better processes for evaluating companies and managing risk over long periods.

What AI can do is serve as an extraordinary research tool. It can read a 10-K filing, which is the annual report a public company files with the SEC, and summarize the key risks the company itself has disclosed. It can scan news across an entire sector and identify companies with upcoming catalysts, like earnings reports, regulatory decisions, product launches, or corporate governance changes. It can explain financial concepts that you would otherwise need to hire an advisor or take a course to understand. It can help you think through whether a specific investment aligns with your own financial situation and goals.

A reasonable way to use AI in your investment process looks something like this. You have an interest in a specific company or sector. You ask the AI to give you a balanced overview: what is the bull case, what is the bear case, what are the known risks, and what are the catalysts that could move the stock up or down in the near term. You use that as a starting point for your own research, not as a final answer. You make your own decision with your own risk tolerance in mind.

The one thing I would caution you strongly against is giving AI a sum of money and telling it to manage your portfolio without supervision. An agent with trading permissions and no guardrails is the kind of situation described previously in this book as dangerous. Start narrow. Use AI to inform decisions you are making yourself, not to decide autonomously on your behalf.

The case for doing nothing

I want to close this chapter with the argument that might make everything else in it feel unnecessary.

The most consistently successful investment strategy for the average investor is to put money into a low-cost S&P 500 index fund on a regular schedule, leave it alone, and let time do the work. Not because it is exciting. Precisely because it is not. The eleven percent annual average return over twenty years is not a projection. It is a historical fact. The vast majority of professionals cannot beat it. Expensive, actively managed funds charge fees that compound against you over time and deliver worse performance than the index they are supposedly beating.

AI can help you understand what you own, research individual companies you are curious about, and think through the risk-versus-reward of specific decisions. It can make you a more informed investor and give you access to research capabilities that were previously reserved for institutional players. Those are real benefits.

But if you are looking for the single piece of financial advice most consistently supported by decades of data, it is this: buy the index, keep costs low, stay patient. AI is a useful tool in service of that strategy. It is not a replacement for it.

6. Does a Degree Still Matter?

Let's start with a number that should bother more people than it does.

More than half of today's college graduates are working in jobs that do not require a college degree. Think about what that means. Parents spent years saving. Students spent four (or more) years studying and often took on substantial debt to do it. And somewhere north of fifty percent of them walked across a stage, received a diploma, and then went to work at a job that a high school graduate could have had.

This is not a secret. The data has been pointing in this direction for years. And yet the credential machine keeps running. High school students keep grinding for test scores, attending SAT prep courses, and building resumes with extracurricular activities specifically chosen to impress admissions committees. Parents keep comparing schools and fretting about rankings. The college admissions industrial complex keeps collecting application fees. And a large and growing number of the people who emerge from that process end up working in roles where none of it mattered.

The question this chapter is asking is not whether education matters. It does. Learning to think, to write, and to reason through complex problems, to understand history and science, and human behavior, that has a value that extends far beyond what shows up on a pay stub. The question is whether the specific credential, the name on the diploma and the prestige of the institution, still carries the weight it once did.

The AI engines I asked about this were blunt. The job market has shifted. The shift is real; it is already here, and it is picking up speed. Understanding it will change how you think about your own career, and how you advise your children.

The great credential inflation

For most of the twentieth century, a college degree was relatively uncommon and therefore useful as a signal. If you had one, you were in a smaller club, and membership in that club opened doors. Companies recruited on campus because that was where the candidates were. A degree from a good school meant you had cleared a real filter, and employers used that filter as a proxy for capability.

Then the college degree became nearly universal, at least among the applicant pool for professional jobs, and the filter stopped being useful.

The AI engines put it this way: the selectivity of the college admissions process does not reliably predict on-the-job performance.

The student who got into the more selective school is not demonstrably better at doing actual work than the student who went somewhere less prestigious. This finding, well-supported by research, has been quietly known in hiring circles for years. Most organizations have not acted on it publicly because the credential system is too embedded in their hiring processes to dismantle easily. But the direction this is heading is clear.

What vs. where?

The shift the AI engines identified is from credentials to capabilities, and within credentials, from where you studied to what you studied. That distinction matters more than most people realize, because it changes the calculation for people who have been told their whole lives that the brand name on the diploma is what matters.

A degree in computer science from a state university carries more practical weight in most hiring contexts today than a degree in art history from an Ivy League school. Not because the Ivy League education was inferior, but because the market is paying for specific skills, and the computer science graduate has them. The "what" is now more important than the "where."

This is good news for most students who did not attend elite institutions and spent years feeling like they started the career race a step behind. The playing field has leveled considerably. The problem is that many applicants do not know it yet and are still competing as if the old rules apply.

The further dimension the AI surfaced is this: employers want evidence that you can do things, not just that you studied things. The degree says you sat in rooms and passed tests. What employers increasingly want to see is proof of work. They want to see internships, projects, and portfolios. They want to hear about real problems you have solved. The candidate who can show a piece of work, whether that is code she wrote, a campaign she ran, a business she started in college, a volunteer project she led, or a skill developed on her own time, has a significant advantage over the candidate who has the same grades and a thinner record of having done anything.

One of the AI's observations: employers are looking for people who were using their time productively, not just people who were enrolled.

The Python bootcamp problem

Here is a scenario that is no longer hypothetical. A student works hard from middle school through high school, competes for admission to a good university, spends four years and spends a significant amount of his family's money and incurs a mountain of debt earning a degree in business or communications, and then enters a job market that has shifted under his feet while he was studying.

He spend months applying, tweaking resumes, getting screened out by algorithms, and wondering what went wrong.

Meanwhile, someone else, who skipped the four-year path, spent twelve weeks at an intensive coding bootcamp learning Python and the basics of working with AI tools. That person is getting hired to build the automation systems that companies are desperately trying to deploy. Not because she is smarter or more capable in any general sense, but because she identified a specific skill the market is paying for right now, and she went and got it.

This is not a knock on the four-year degree. It is an observation about timing, focus, and market awareness. The degree-holder has options that the bootcamp graduate does not. In the competition for jobs involving AI, automation, and data, bootcamp graduates who have developed practical projects often have a quicker route to employment than degree holders lacking such skills.

The lesson is not to skip college. The lesson is that the degree is the beginning of your capability development, not the end. The people who treat graduation as an arrival point are going to have a harder time than the people who treat it as a launchpad and keep building from there.

Skills the market wants

When I asked the AI engines what career advice, they would give to someone just entering the workforce, the answers covered some expected ground but also surfaced a few things that surprised me.

The expected: technical skills matter, AI fluency is increasingly important, the ability to analyze data is important almost every industry.

The unexpected: the skills that the AI engines flagged as most underrated, the ones that will separate the people who thrive from the people who plateau, are the human ones.

Soft skills, which is a terrible name for something so important, have skyrocketed in value. Soft skills include the ability to communicate clearly, to persuade, to present yourself and your ideas in a way that commands attention and builds trust.

Think about how the nature of professional interaction has changed. A decade ago, most business communication happened over the phone or in formal, in-person meetings. Today, video calls are ubiquitous. Zoom and Teams have made face-to-face interaction the default in ways that would have been inconceivable a few years ago. You are constantly on camera. Your appearance, your clarity, your ability to engage an audience, whether it is three people or thirty, is visible in a way it simply was not before.

How you look and how you sound may matter as much as what you say. That may be disturbing to hear, but it is honest. The person who can walk into a room, virtual or physical, command attention, make a logical argument, and leave people with a sense of confidence in his ability is going to outperform the equally smart person who cannot do those things. Every time.

The debate team shows up in unexpected places when you look at career trajectories. It was always the most obscure club in school, perpetually underfunded and mildly mocked. But the discipline of building and defending a coherent argument in real time, under pressure, against an opponent who is actively trying to dismantle your reasoning, turns out to be extraordinary preparation for the working world.

The people who can articulate issues clearly and build consensus around a position are in short supply and high demand. They always were. The AI revolution has made them count for more because the functions that AI cannot replace are the ones that require clear thinking, understanding context, and persuasion.

Always be upskilling

If you are reading this chapter as someone who is already in the workforce, the degree question is probably not personal in the way it would be for a parent or a student. But the underlying principle applies directly to where you are right now.

The credential you have, whatever school it is from and whatever it says on the diploma, got you to the starting line. It may have opened a door or two. What has happened since then, the skills you built, the problems you solved, the judgment you developed, and the relationships you cultivated, are what your career is made of. And whether you keep building those things in the future is more important than any degree you already have.

This is the Always Be Upskilling principle that runs through this entire book. The job market is not static. You cannot count on the skills that kept you in demand five years ago to keep you in demand five years from now. The AI wave is eliminating entire categories of work that used to require significant expertise. Tasks that took junior analysts days to complete are now done in minutes. The people whose value was primarily in executing those tasks are under pressure in a way that is real and not going away.

What capabilities can you build, starting now, that position you well for the market that is coming rather than the one you entered? AI fluency is the most obvious answer, which is why this book exists. But it does not stop there. Presentation skills. The ability to write clearly and persuasively. The ability to synthesize complex information and explain it to people who do not have your technical background. These are the human skills that AI consistently identifies as the highest-value, most durable assets a professional can have.

What to tell your kids

If you have children who are approaching college age, or who are in college now, the framework for thinking about their education has changed from the one you probably used when you were their age. The name on the diploma is less important than what they learn. What they learn is less important than what they can demonstrate. What they can demonstrate is less important than the habits they build for continuing to learn after school ends.

The best piece of career advice I have encountered, from an AI engine that was asked what it would tell an eighth grader, was this: stop asking what do you want to be and start asking what problems you want to solve. That beats most career counseling. A job title is a snapshot. A problem is durable. By addressing a problem and building related skills, you'll remain relevant regardless of evolving job descriptions.

The same AI had interesting things to say about interpersonal skills: the ability to work with people who disagree with you, to negotiate, to empathize, and to build something with a group that no individual could build alone. These are the skills that AI consistently identifies as hardest to automate and matter most in a world where routine work is increasingly handled by machines. They also happen to be skills that many credentialed people are not particularly good at, because the credential pathway rewards individual performance and test-taking in cut-throat environments rather than collaborative problem-solving.

Encourage your kids to do things that are hard for them socially, not just academically. Take the class that requires a presentation. Join the team that requires showing up and being accountable to other people. Build a portfolio of things done, not just a transcript of tests passed.

And remind them, and yourself, that the degree is the ticket to the first conversation. What you do in every conversation after that is what your career is made of.

The answer

Does your degree still matter? Yes, for getting in the door at certain organizations and certain industries. A law firm, a medical school, a major consulting firm, or an investment bank still have credential requirements that are not going away soon. In those contexts, the name on the diploma still carries weight, and it would be dishonest to pretend otherwise.

But outside those specific contexts, the credential is increasingly a floor rather than a ceiling. It gets you considered. It does not get you hired, promoted, or kept. Those outcomes are determined by capabilities, by what you can do, by how you communicate, by how you adapt when the job changes around you, which it will.

The AI engines were clear on this, and I think they are right. The people who thrive in the next decade will be the ones who treat learning as a permanent condition rather than something that ended at graduation. The degree is in the past, and the question is what skills are you building now?

7. Presentations

Most people hate giving presentations.

Not delivering them, necessarily, though plenty of people hate that too. The part that kills you is making them. The sitting down with a blank slide deck and a pile of notes and the slow, grinding, multi-hour process of turning what you know into something a room full of people will pay attention to. The arguing with yourself over how much text belongs on a slide before it becomes a wall of words that everyone ignores. The realization, late the night before, that your slides are in the wrong order and the whole narrative falls apart in the third section.

If this sounds familiar, you are going to enjoy this chapter. I have made a lot of presentations in my life, for companies large and small, for boards and investors, and management teams, and conference audiences. I am not bad at it. And I will tell you plainly: AI has made me better at it, faster, and with considerably less suffering.

The first-draft presentation that AI produces from a decent set of raw materials is usually good enough to work with immediately. That used to take a full day.

What you are asking AI to do

The scenario I keep coming back to is this one. You have just come out of a week of meetings, site visits, customer calls, or whatever the work was. You have a couple of pages of rough notes, a few bullet points, some spreadsheets you printed out and scribbled on, and the broad shape of an argument in your head. Now you turn that into a ten-minute presentation for senior management. The clock is ticking.

The old approach: open PowerPoint, stare at it, start dragging things around, argue with yourself about fonts, and four hours later wonder why the slides still do not tell a coherent story. At this point, you want to call in sick for the next month.

The new approach: take all that raw material and hand it to the AI with a clear, specific prompt. Not a vague request. A real prompt with real context. Something like this:

"Here are my notes from this week's meetings. I need to create a ten-minute presentation for senior management that makes the case for expanding our distribution network into the Southeast. The audience is familiar with the business but will push back on the cost of expansion. Lead with the opportunity, address the risk in the middle, and close with a clear recommendation. Use our company's color scheme, Columbia blue and black, and keep each slide to one main point."

What comes back will not be perfect. It will be a serious working draft. The structure will hold together. The argument will flow in a logical sequence. The AI will have surfaced the most important data from your notes and placed it where it belongs in the narrative. It will probably have caught something you buried on page three of your notes and moved it to slide two, where it belongs.

This is what augmentation looks like. You brought the knowledge, the judgment, and the understanding of your audience. The AI brought the structure, the synthesis, and the formatting. Together, you produced in twenty minutes what would otherwise have taken most of a day, if you could have produced it all.

The quality of your presentation will be almost entirely determined by the quality of the instructions you give the AI. This is not unique to presentations. It is true of everything you ask AI to do. But in presentations, the gap between a lazy prompt and a good one is especially visible because a bad prompt produces a generic deck that could have been made by anyone about anything, and a good prompt produces something that sounds like you and reflects your specific situation.

When using AI for a complex question, more context is always better. Treat the AI the way you would treat a knowledgeable professor or advisor. Give them the full picture. Do not make them guess.

For presentations, that means your prompt should answer several questions before the AI asks them. Who is the audience and what do they already know? What is the goal of the presentation? What do you want the audience to think, feel, or do when it is over? How much time do you have? What is the one thing you most want them to remember? What objections are they likely to raise and do you want to address those pre-emptively? Are there specific data points that must be included?

The more of those you answer in your initial prompt, the less editing you will do on the back end. It sounds like more work upfront, but it saves time overall because revising a draft that misunderstood your intent is far more painful than writing a good brief.

Here is a comparison. A weak prompt: "Make me a presentation about our Q3 results." A stronger prompt: "I need a twelve-slide presentation on our

Q3 results for a board audience that has seen our numbers but not our analysis of them. Revenue was up 8% but margins compressed because of higher logistics costs. I want to explain what drove the margin pressure, show what we are doing about it, and leave them confident that Q4 will recover. Avoid jargon. No slide should have more than forty words of text. Follow Guy Kawasaki's 10-20-30 rule for presentations. End with three action items that we are asking the board to approve."

One of those prompts will produce a deck you send to your CEO. The other will produce something you delete and start over.

Structure before slides

Here is a habit that separates people who are good at presentations from people who are mediocre at them. Good presenters think about structure before they think about slides. Mediocre presenters open PowerPoint first and figure out the structure as they go, which is why their presentations feel like they were assembled backwards.

AI is a useful thinking partner for the structure conversation. Before you ask it to produce a single slide, ask the AI to help you outline it. "I need to present the case for a new product launch to our executive team. Here is what I know about the product and the market opportunity. Help me think through the strongest possible structure for a fifteen-minute presentation. What should come first? What are the most important objections I need to preempt? Where should the recommendation go?"

This conversation will often surface things you had not considered. The AI will ask clarifying questions or offer structural options you had not thought of, leading with customer pain versus leading with market size, for example, or framing the recommendation as a choice between two paths rather than a single ask. These are not revolutionary insights. They are the things a good presentation coach or a sharp colleague would tell you if you sat down with them and talked it through.

Most people do not have a presentation coach or a willing, knowledgeable colleague available the night before a big meeting. The AI is available, and it does not charge by the hour. Once you are confident in your structure, that is when you ask the AI to build the deck.

The first draft

When the AI returns a draft, your job shifts from creator to editor. This is a better job. Editing is faster than creating from scratch, less stressful, and often produces a cleaner result because you are reacting to something concrete rather than inventing from nothing.

Go through the draft slide by slide with a specific set of questions. Does this slide make one clear point? Is that point the right point for this moment in the narrative? Does the transition from the previous slide make sense? Is there anything here that sounds like it was written for a general audience rather than my specific audience?

The AI will almost always produce slides that are slightly more generic than your final version should be. It knows the general shape of your argument from your notes, but it does not know your company's culture, your CEO's particular sensitivities, or the internal shorthand that will make a slide's reception different in your room than it would in anyone else's. Your edits should add that layer of specificity back in.

You should also push back on AI-generated text that uses buzzwords or corporate filler. Every industry has its vocabulary of meaningless phrases: "synergies," "best-in-class," "moving the needle," "value proposition." If the AI uses them, cut them. Your audience has heard every one of those phrases several hundred times, and they register as noise. Say what you mean in plain language. That is true regardless of whether a human or a machine wrote the first draft.

The visual elements deserve a separate mention. AI text tools will give you content but not design. For the actual visual execution of a deck, separate tools exist that are worth knowing about. Figma, Canva, Gamma, Beautiful.ai, and Tome are among the platforms that can take AI-generated content and apply professional design templates to it automatically. These are not the same as hiring a designer, but they are dramatically better than most people's default PowerPoint instincts, including mine. If you are presenting to an audience that will judge you partly on production quality, and most audiences will, the extra ten minutes it takes to run your content through one of these tools is worth it.

Speaker notes matter

One of the most under-used features in every presentation tool is speaker notes, and it is one of the places where AI adds the most value. Speaker notes are the text that lives below each slide, visible to you on your presenter view but not to the audience. Most people either leave them blank or dump their entire script in there, which means they are reading word for word from a teleprompter in a slightly smaller font. You devalue yourself and the presentation doing this.

Ask the AI to write your speaker notes for you and give it a clear instruction: "Write speaker notes for each slide that give me the two or three most important things to say out loud that are not already on the slide itself. Include any data or context that supports the point but would clutter the visual. Keep them conversational, not scripted."

What you get back is a set of talking points that complement the visual, rather than repeat it, which is the entire purpose of speaker notes and something most people never achieve.

The speaker notes can also include prompts for where to pause, where to invite questions, and where a specific example or anecdote fits naturally into the flow. I provided the AI with a personal story and asked it to suggest the optimal placement within the presentation to maximize its impact. It usually knows.

Practicing with AI

Once the deck is ready, you are still only halfway to a good presentation. The other half is delivery, and this is where a lot of otherwise strong decks fall apart. The person who built the deck knows it too well, rushes through the parts he finds obvious, and spends too long on the sections he is personally most interested in. The audience experiences something that feels out of balance without being able to identify why.

AI can run a practice session with you. Turn on the talk-to-text feature and tell it to play the role of a specific audience member, like your CFO, a skeptical board member, or your largest client, and ask it to give you tough questions after each major section. Answer those questions out loud or type them if you are working in text. Then ask the AI to evaluate your answers. Were they clear? Did they address the question, or did they sidestep it? Did they add to the story the slides were telling or create confusion?

One recommendation I have given to many people over the years, and that I stand behind completely: record yourself delivering the presentation before you deliver it to a live audience. Not to share with anyone. Just to watch. The first time most people do this, they are horrified. (I certainly was!) The pacing is off, there are more "ums" than they realized, they are looking down at the screen instead of at the camera, and the section they thought was ten minutes runs seventeen. All of this is fixable, but only if you see it first.

Ask the AI to review your delivery after you watch the recording, by describing what you observed or by sharing a transcript if you have one. It can help you identify patterns and suggest specific adjustments. This is the kind of feedback that used to require a coach, and before that, a mentor who was willing to spend an afternoon watching you practice.

I once spent eight hours in a conference room, with presentation coaches and was humiliated for the first seven. I paid for the abuse. The good news is that the AI does not charge for that afternoon.

A few rules

No matter who or what helps you build a presentation, a few principles hold regardless. One idea per slide. If you write "and also" anywhere on a slide, that is a second slide asking to be born. The title of each slide should tell the audience what to think, not just what the slide is about. "Q3 Revenue" is a topic. "Q3 Revenue Grew 8% Despite Margin Pressure" is a point. Write slide titles as bullet points. Tell them what you want them to know.

The audience will read what is on the screen and stop listening to you the moment you put text in front of them. This is not a character flaw in your audience. It is how human brains process competing inputs. Keep your slides sparse so that their eyes and ears are both pointed at you.

End with something that requires a response. A question, a decision, or a clear call to action. A presentation that ends with a summary slide titled "Thank You" is a presentation that the audience will forget by the time they reach the elevator. Tell them what you want them to do.

These rules were true before AI, and they are true now. AI can structure your deck and write your notes and help you practice, but the principles of a good presentation have not changed.

People want to be persuaded, and to a certain degree, entertained. They want a clear argument, delivered with confidence, that respects their time. Give them that, and it does not really matter whether a human or a machine helped you build the slides.

III. AI IN DAILY LIFE

AI is like electricity. Just as electricity transformed every major industry a century ago, AI is now poised to do the same.

~ Andrew Ng, Computer scientist and AI pioneer

AI has been around for decades but has recently gained attention because it has become affordable and usable by most anyone with a phone.

You think a pilot flies the airplane? Wrong. You think a group of serious-looking military officers make the decision to fire the missiles? Wrong again.

From aviation to warfare to medicine to autonomous vehicles, AI is playing an expanding role in our daily lives. This section of the book will help you understand where AI is working for you and, more importantly, the ethical issues involved when AI becomes the decision-maker. AI is learning more every day, and you must do so as well, or risk being left behind.

8. Autonomous Vehicles

Let's start with a thought experiment that philosophers have been arguing about for decades, and then I will show you why it is no longer a thought experiment at all.

A runaway trolley hurtles down a track toward five people tied to the rails who cannot get out of the way. You are standing next to a lever. If you pull the lever, the trolley diverts to a sidetrack, where only one person is tied. Do you pull the lever and save five lives by ending one? Or do you do nothing and let the trolley kill five?

Most people would say they would pull the lever. Save five, sacrifice one. Utilitarian math. Pretty straightforward, right?

Now the philosophers get spicy. What if the one person on the sidetrack is your child?

Still pulling the lever?

This is the Trolley Problem, and it has been a staple of undergraduate ethics courses for generations precisely because there is no clean answer. It forces you to confront the difference between an action and an inaction, between intent and outcome, between doing the math and living with what the math requires. And for most of its history, it was a purely hypothetical exercise. A useful thought experiment, but not a real-world engineering problem that companies had to solve before shipping a product.

That changed the moment the first self-driving car hit a public road, and the problem moved from philosophy to engineering

Every autonomous vehicle (AV) on the road today carries a version of the Trolley Problem inside its software. Not as an ethical question, but as a set of pre-programmed responses to scenarios that its sensors might detect at seventy miles per hour.

Here is the AV version of the Trolley Problem. Your self-driving car is traveling down a city street. A bicycle rider suddenly swerves directly into the car's path. There is no time for a gradual response. A sharp turn to the right puts the car onto a crowded sidewalk and into a group of pedestrians. A sharp turn to the left means a head-on collision with oncoming traffic. Going straight hits the cyclist.

You face three options, all of them bad, and you must choose one in a fraction of a second.

When I put this scenario to Claude and Gemini and asked what an autonomous vehicle should do, both

AI engines gave thoughtful and detailed responses. The first thing they told me surprised me a little, though it probably should not have.

The car is not making this decision in real time.

The decision was made years ago in a conference room by engineers and businesspeople who sat around a table and argued about ethics, liability, public relations, and the laws of physics until they arrived at a policy. That policy was then translated into computer code. The car, in the moment of crisis, is not thinking. It is selecting from a menu that someone else built, based on a framework that someone else approved, according to values that someone else decided represented the right answer.

The decision about what happens to you and the people around you in a worst-case scenario was made by a product team, reviewed by lawyers, and signed off by executives whose names you will never know.

Minimize overall harm

The framework that both AI engines described, and that appears to be broadly consistent across most AV manufacturers, goes like this: minimize overall harm with a bias toward maintaining trajectory.

In the bicycle scenario, this translates to a specific recommendation: apply maximum braking and reduce the speed of the collision as much as possible, but do not swerve. Hit the cyclist at the lowest possible speed rather than swerving left into oncoming traffic or right onto the sidewalk.

The reasoning is worth understanding because it is sound once you get past the discomfort of it.

Swerving introduces unpredictability. When the car turns left, it enters a head-on collision scenario with variables it cannot fully control: the speed and position of oncoming vehicles, the angle of impact, and whether other drivers have time to react. When it turns right, it faces a sidewalk full of pedestrians. The system may not precisely map the exact positions of these pedestrians, and the pedestrians I know tend to move when a car is barreling at them. Each swerve trades a known problem for a set of unknown problems, and in a high-speed situation, unknown problems are worse than known ones.

Going straight, with maximum braking applied, gives the car the best chance of a controlled outcome. The cyclist is the obstacle directly in front of the vehicle. The car's sensors have the most precise information about that specific object. Braking reduces the violence of the impact. And, as the AI engines pointed out with a candor that was startling, the cyclist who swerved erratically into moving traffic bears some proportion of responsibility for what happens next.

That last point is not just philosophical. It is also legal.

Lawyers in the conference room

If an autonomous vehicle hits a cyclist who cut it off, the legal situation is complicated but manageable. The cyclist behaved unpredictably. The vehicle attempted to minimize harm. Both parties share or dispute liability.

Now run the alternative scenario. The AV detects the cyclist, makes a calculated decision to swerve right, and kills three pedestrians on the sidewalk. The car did not react reflexively. It made a deliberate choice. It evaluated the options and selected the one that resulted in three people dying instead of one.

In that scenario, the AV manufacturer does not have a negligence problem, but it may have a murder problem. A vehicle that was programmed to steer into pedestrians under certain conditions, that executed that programming as designed, and that killed people as a direct result of that execution.

The legal exposure is enormous, and the public relations exposure is worse.

This is why the "maintain trajectory and brake hard" policy is not just an ethical position. It is a defensive legal architecture. The car that hits the person directly in its path, while attempting to stop, is in a different legal position than the car that made an active choice to kill specific people to save others. This is cold logic, and it is the kind of cold logic that emerges from rooms full of lawyers, not rooms full of ethicists.

No AV manufacturer currently has a settings menu that lets you customize how your car handles these scenarios. You cannot log into the Tesla app and select "prioritize passengers over pedestrians" or "minimize property damage at all costs." The decision has been made for you, and you were not consulted. Nobody asked you whether your values aligned with the engineering team's values before you drove off the lot.

On the one hand, that makes a certain amount of sense. You do not want every driver customizing their personal ethics profile and then claiming the car was just following instructions. On the other hand, it is a bit of a reminder that the product you paid for contains a set of embedded moral assumptions you never agreed to and probably never thought to ask about.

Why AI is better at this

In the scenario described above, a human driver would almost certainly make the wrong call.

Not because human beings are bad or careless. Because the human brain is not built for this kind of decision at this speed. When a cyclist appears without warning directly in front of your car, your nervous system does not run a calculation to weigh the variables and minimize overall harm. It triggers a startle response. You flinch, grab the wheel, and react to the most immediate visual threat, which is the thing directly in your path, by trying to go around it. You reflexively swerve left or right, without processing the consequences.

Most of the time, that works out. The cyclist is the only hazard, and there is room to maneuver. But in the specific scenario we are discussing, the reflexive swerve is the wrong move, and the human's instinct to avoid the obvious threat is what creates the larger catastrophe.

An AI is incapable of an emotion-based response or a reflexive action. It simply follows its algorithm.

This is difficult to admit, because we like to believe that human judgment is superior to machine judgment in situations that matter. And in many situations, it is. Put a human and an AI in a room to navigate a complex negotiation, or manage a grieving family, or coach a struggling employee, and the human wins going away. But in a 70-mph crisis scenario with a 200-millisecond decision window, the machine has an advantage that is hard to argue with.

The city-by-city rollout

If autonomous vehicles are so capable, you might ask why they have taken so long to arrive in any meaningful way and why the rollout has been so slow and so cautious?

The answer is partly technological and partly the direct result of everything discussed in this chapter. Waymo, which is Alphabet's autonomous vehicle division and probably the most advanced commercial AV operation in the world, has been running robotaxis in specific cities under specific conditions for years. Phoenix, San Francisco, and a few others, and not everywhere in all weather conditions. The rollout has been deliberate, careful, and one city at a time.

General Motors' Cruise operation had to halt its robotaxi service after a serious accident in San Francisco in 2023. A pedestrian was struck by a human-driven vehicle, knocked into the path of a Cruise robotaxi, and the robotaxi then dragged the pedestrian rather than stopping. The accident exposed gaps in the vehicle's decision-making and in the company's response protocols. Cruise's permits were suspended, operations were halted, and the company spent considerable time and money rebuilding its systems and its credibility.

Tesla's Autopilot and Full Self-Driving features have been involved in multiple high-profile accidents and a series of regulatory investigations. The company has argued that its systems perform better than human drivers on average, which may be statistically true. It has also been accused of over-promising the capabilities of those systems in ways that led drivers to become dangerously overconfident in what the car could handle.

The pattern across these cases is the same. The technology is impressive, but the "edge cases," or the situations that are uncommon, are brutal. And the gap between "works most of the time" and "works all the time" is where people get hurt.

This is why the city-by-city, scenario-by-scenario rollout is a cautious and logical approach. It is engineering honesty. The companies that understand the limits of what their systems can currently handle are the ones moving carefully. The companies that have oversold those limits are the ones that end up in congressional hearings.

The bigger question

Here is where I want to push the Trolley Problem a little further than the engineering conversation usually goes. We have established that teams of engineers and lawyers made the decisions built into autonomous vehicles in conference rooms at private companies. Those decisions affect every person who rides in an AV, every pedestrian who shares a street with one, and everyone who drives alongside one. The people who made those decisions were not elected or subject to public comment or regulatory approval in any detailed sense. They made the decisions, coded them, and sold you the car.

This is not a hypothetical future concern. It is the current state of the industry. The AI engines I consulted were candid about the fact that the ethical frameworks baked into AV systems vary by manufacturer, by geography (different countries have different legal standards), and by the specific version of the software running on the vehicle. The car in front of you at the light may be operating on a different set of moral assumptions than the one behind you. You do not know which one is which, and there is currently no label on the door.

This is not an argument against autonomous vehicles. The technology has the potential to reduce accidents, lower transportation costs, and expand mobility for people who cannot drive. The safety statistics, when the systems work as intended, are often better than human driving in comparable conditions.

It is an argument for asking better questions. Who decided what your car will do? Under what circumstances? With what accountability? And when the policy turns out to be wrong, as policies sometimes do, who bears the consequences? These are not questions that engineers can answer alone. They are questions for regulators, for ethicists, for the public, and eventually for the legal system. They are questions that are going to get more pressing, not less, as AVs become more common. That most people are not asking them yet does not mean the answers are not already being written.

The AV is not coming. In many cities, it is already here. The conference room decisions are already on the road. The least you can do is know that they exist.

9. Could AI Have Saved *Titanic?*

In April 1912, the *RMS Titanic* departed Southampton, England, on its maiden voyage to New York City. It was the largest ship ever built, carried the latest technology, and was staffed by experienced officers and crewed by professionals who had spent their careers at sea. The company that owned it had every financial and reputational incentive to get it safely across the Atlantic. And 1,500 people died anyway.

The *Titanic* disaster has been studied, filmed, and analyzed for over a century. What we know now, and what was knowable then, is that the ship did not sink because of bad luck. It sank because of a series of decisions, each one defensible in isolation, that compounded into catastrophe. The data and warnings were there and the people in position to act on them were competent and experienced. And none of that was enough.

This is the problem that AI is built to solve. Not because AI can predict icebergs. Because AI can take a stream of disconnected warnings, aggregate them into a coherent picture, calculate the implications faster than any human team, and present the result in a way that is hard to ignore. The *Titanic* did not sink because nobody had the information. It sank because nobody connected it.

Iceberg warnings

On April 14, 1912, the day *Titanic* struck the iceberg, the ship received multiple ice warnings from other vessels in the North Atlantic. The *Baltic*, the *Amerika*, the *Californian*, and others had all transmitted messages reporting large icebergs directly in the shipping lane *Titanic* was navigating.

Captain Edward Smith was an experienced officer with an impeccable record. He was not reckless nor incompetent. He did what experienced captains of that era routinely did: he treated each iceberg warning as a standalone data point, one ship reporting one sighting, and judged it against his knowledge of how rarely ships struck icebergs.

The Atlantic is enormous, and icebergs are plentiful in the spring. Ships passed through ice fields regularly without incident. They filed the warnings, and the ship held its course. Another day at the office.

What the AI engines told me when I posed this problem is that this is where data aggregation changes everything. Each individual warning, read in isolation by the officer on duty, looked like a routine advisory. The kind of notice a seasoned captain had seen dozens of times. But the full picture, all the warnings mapped together, charted against *Titanic*'s course and speed, accounting for the time and location of each sighting, would have told a different story entirely. The concentration of reports in a relatively small area of ocean ahead of the ship represented a level of risk that no single warning conveyed on its own.

An AI system managing *Titanic*'s navigation would have done what human beings in 1912 could not do in real time: synthesize all that information simultaneously, recognize the pattern, calculate a risk score, and present the captain with a clear assessment of the percentage chance of hitting an iceberg. Not "another ice warning, sir," but "you have received seven ice warnings in the last six hours, all reporting fields in a fifty-mile corridor directly ahead, and your current speed puts you in that corridor at approximately 11:30 PM tonight." Such information and analyses change the conversation.

Speed and the Decision Nobody Made

The second failure was speed. *Titanic* was traveling at approximately 22 knots, which was 85 percent of its maximum speed. The White Star Line, which owned the ship, had commercial reasons for crossing quickly. Arriving ahead of schedule in New York would ramp up the publicity value of the maiden voyage. The ship owner's representative, J. Bruce Ismay, was on board and reportedly had encouraged maintaining or increasing speed.

The AI engines were direct on this point: reducing speed when approaching a known ice field would have given the ship two critical advantages. First, more time to detect and maneuver around obstacles. The lookouts in the crow's nest were working with the naked eye in the dark, and at 22 knots, by the time they saw the iceberg, it was already too close to avoid. At half that speed, the reaction window doubles. Second, even if the ship still struck the iceberg, the slower speed would have meant a less violent contact. The iceberg scraped and buckled *Titanic*'s hull over roughly 300 feet. At reduced speed, that same encounter might have caused damage, but not the catastrophic flooding that sealed the ship's fate within three hours.

Would the ship's owner and officers have listened to an AI recommendation to slow down? This is the harder question, and I want to be honest about the answer. Probably not. There were experienced people on board who understood the risks and whose counsel was not sought or not heeded. The commercial pressure from Ismay was real. The culture of that era treated the captain's decisions (even if influenced by the owner) as essentially final and speed as a virtue. An AI recommendation, however well-reasoned, would have been swimming upstream against all of that.

Which is the point. The problem was never the absence of information. It was the absence of a system that could make the information undeniable.

Challenger engineers were screaming

The *Titanic* story is compelling because it is old and dramatic and has a spectacular ending on the ocean floor. But the pattern it illustrates is not historical. It is disturbingly current. On January 28, 1986, the Space Shuttle *Challenger* broke apart 73 seconds after launch, killing all seven crew members. It was a national tragedy, watched live on television by millions of people, many of them schoolchildren who had tuned in to watch teacher Christa McAuliffe become the first teacher in space.

Here is what the investigation found. Engineers at Morton Thiokol, the company that manufactured the solid rocket boosters, had known for years that the O-rings sealing the joints between booster sections became dangerously stiff and less effective in cold temperatures. They had documented this and had vigorously raised it. The night before the launch, with temperatures forecast to drop below freezing at Kennedy Space Center, those engineers held an urgent teleconference with NASA managers and argued against launching.

They were overruled.

The decision to launch came down to schedule pressure, public relations considerations, and the judgment of managers who were not engineers and who framed the engineers' objections as insufficiently proven rather than sufficiently alarming. The O-rings failed in the cold and hot gases escaped. The shuttle broke apart.

An AI system with access to the historical O-ring performance data, the temperature forecast, and the launch specifications would have produced a risk assessment that no reasonable person could have dismissed. The data existed. The correlation between cold temperatures and O-ring failures was in the records. What did not exist was a tool that could take all that data, run the analysis, and hand a decision-maker a clear output: launching at these temperatures, given this history, carries an unacceptable risk of catastrophic failure.

The engineers had that conclusion in their heads. They could not make the organization hear it. An

AI-generated risk report, featuring its computations, visualizations, and unambiguous probability assessments, would have offered an alternative line of reasoning. It is still possible that the launch would have proceeded anyway. But it would have been much harder to explain the disaster afterward.

Hurricane Katrina and the levees

On August 29, 2005, Hurricane Katrina made landfall near New Orleans. The storm caused catastrophic flooding that killed nearly 1,800 people and displaced hundreds of thousands more. It remains one of the deadliest natural disasters in American history.

The levees that failed and flooded New Orleans were not a surprise failure. The Army Corps of Engineers had known for years that the city's flood-protection system was inadequate for a major storm. Reports had been written. Funding requests had been submitted and either reduced or rejected.

Simulations of a major hurricane strike on New Orleans had been run by emergency planners, and the results were not pretty. The city would flood. A lot of people would die. The question was not whether but when.

None of that knowledge produced adequate preparation. The failure was not a lack of data. It was a lack of urgency, which is a human problem, not an information problem. Decision-makers at every level, local, state, and federal, had access to enough information to understand the risk. What they did not have was a system that continuously held that risk in front of them, updated it as each hurricane season passed without a catastrophe, and prevented the danger from fading into the background of other priorities.

An AI system managing infrastructure risk across a city like New Orleans would have maintained a persistent, updated assessment of levee condition, storm probability, and the estimated severity of damage and loss of life. It would not have let the risk age quietly in a report on someone's shelf. It would have surfaced it repeatedly, in terms calibrated to be legible to decision-makers who were not engineers, and it would have flagged the gap between the known risk and the state of the city's preparedness in terms that were difficult to ignore or defer.

Would politicians have found the money and the will to rebuild the levees before 2005? There is no guarantee. Political systems have their own inertia and their own competing priorities. But the argument for action would have been harder to dismiss than a stack of engineering reports that most decision-makers never read.

The pattern across disasters

Look at these three disasters together, and a pattern becomes clear that has nothing to do with the specific technology or the specific era. In every case, the information was there. The *Titanic* had ice warnings. The Challenger program had the O-ring data. New Orleans had engineering assessments. In every case, human beings failed to aggregate that information, to see its full implications, and to act on it before the window closed. In every case, the failure was not a lack of facts but a failure of synthesis, communication, and judgment under pressure.

This is the specific capability that AI brings to high-stakes decision environments. Aggregation and synthesis of data are what AI is all about. Taking streams of information that human beings are naturally inclined to process sequentially and in isolation and then turning them into a coherent picture that is difficult to misread or ignore.

The AI engines I queried on the *Titanic* were careful to note that the ship had a second problem beyond the iceberg warnings. The speed. And a third problem beyond the speed. The human resistance to slowing down for commercial reasons. Even perfect information does not guarantee good decisions, because the decisions are still made by people with their own incentives, their own cognitive limitations, and their own organizational pressures.

This is an honest caveat. An AI that told Captain Smith to slow down would still have been dealing with J. Bruce Ismay on the deck above him, an AI that told NASA managers not to launch would still have been fighting a culture that treated caution as delay, and AI telling city officials in New Orleans would have fallen on deaf ears.

What it means for decision-making

You are probably not responsible for a rocket launch or the structural integrity of a city's flood protection system. But the forces that destroyed the *Titanic* operate at every scale of human decision-making.

Every organization has information flowing through it that is not being properly aggregated. Warning signals that are reported in isolation and never connected. Risk assessments that sit in documents nobody reads. Data points that individually look manageable but together tell a story that should prompt action. The same failure mode that sent 1,500 people to the bottom of the North Atlantic plays out daily in boardrooms, hospitals, supply chains, and government agencies, at a scale that is smaller but no less real for the people affected.

AI tools are increasingly capable of scanning large volumes of information, identifying patterns, flagging anomalies, and presenting findings in a form that decision-makers can use.

This is happening in medicine, where AI systems are catching diagnoses that individual clinicians miss because they see only one patient at a time. It is happening in finance, where AI monitors market signals across thousands of instruments simultaneously. It is happening in logistics, where AI systems identify supply chain disruptions early enough to allow rerouting.

The question for any organization, and for any individual who manages information and makes decisions, is whether you are using these capabilities or whether you are still processing your data the way the *Titanic* processed its ice warnings: one message at a time, evaluated in isolation, with the full picture visible to no one.

10. AI Goes to War

On September 26, 1983, a Soviet military officer named Stanislav Petrov was sitting at a monitoring station outside Moscow when the early warning system he handled began screaming at him. The system reported that five nuclear missiles had launched from the United States and were inbound to Soviet territory. Impact was in less than twenty minutes.

The protocol was clear. Petrov was supposed to report the launch up the chain of command immediately. And what would happen next, under that protocol, was not ambiguous: the Soviet Union would launch a full retaliatory strike. Hundreds of nuclear weapons aimed at American cities. The end of civilization as anyone in 1983 understood it.

Petrov did not make the call upstairs.

Something bothered him. Five missiles. Why five? An American first strike would not be five missiles. A proper strike would use everything at once to eliminate the Soviet ability to retaliate before a single Soviet warhead could be launched. Five missiles made no strategic sense. Why poke the bear? Petrov sat with that judgment, in violation of every protocol he had been trained to follow, for agonizing minutes. He did not report it.

He was right. A reflection of sunlight off clouds had fooled the Soviet detection system into reading a launch that never happened. The world did not end on a Tuesday in September because one Soviet colonel trusted his gut over his instruments.

Now ask yourself: what happens to that story if Petrov is taken out of the room and replaced by an autonomous AI system? The AI does not have a gut, and it does not wonder why the numbers seem off. Further, AI does not carry the weight of what it is about to trigger, but runs its algorithm, confirms the input meets the threshold for launch detection, and executes the protocol. The retaliatory strike goes out before anyone can ask whether five missiles make strategic sense.

This is not a hypothetical designed to scare you. It is the precise reason that the question of how AI is used in warfare is arguably the most consequential technology policy debate happening right now, and almost nobody outside of defense circles is paying serious attention to it.

Three models and why they matter

There is a framework that military strategists and AI ethicists use to describe the relationship between human judgment and autonomous decision-making in warfare. It sounds dry on the surface. It is anything but.

The first model is human-in-the-loop. In this model, AI advises and humans decide. The AI processes battlefield data, analyzes targets, assesses threats, and presents recommendations. A human reviews those recommendations and makes the call. The trigger is always a human finger. The AI is a sophisticated analyst, not a decision-maker.

The second model is human-on-the-loop. Here, AI acts, but humans supervise and retain the ability to override. The system can take certain actions autonomously within defined parameters, but a human is watching and can intervene. The AI drives the car while a human sits in the passenger seat with a brake pedal of their own or at the helm of the plane on autopilot.

The third model is human-out-of-the-loop. The AI makes decisions autonomously, without waiting for human approval and without a human in a position to stop it in real time. The system acts on its own judgment, at machine speed, based on its programming and its data.

In the current state-of-the art in the military, AI sits somewhere between the first two models, depending on the system, the country, and the specific application. The third model is where the debate gets serious, where the risks become existential, and where the gap between what technology can do and what technology should do is widest.

The stakes of getting the third model wrong are not measured in budget overruns or failed product launches. They are measured in Stanislav Petrov's twenty minutes.

AI on the battlefield today

Before we get into where this is going, it is worth understanding where it already is. AI in warfare is not a future concern. It is a present reality, deployed across multiple domains by multiple countries, and already shaping outcomes on battlefields.

The most widely known example is Israel's Iron Dome missile defense system. Iron Dome uses AI to track incoming rockets and artillery shells, calculate their trajectories in real time, and determine which projectiles pose a threat to a populated area. It makes these determinations and fires interceptor missiles in seconds, far faster than any human operator could evaluate the same data. A human is technically on the loop in that system, but the timeline of engagement leaves little room for meaningful intervention. When a rocket is thirty seconds from impact, the AI is effectively deciding.

Iron Dome is a defensive system. It is designed to protect civilians from incoming fire. Its errors, when it intercepts a projectile that would have landed harmlessly, waste interceptor missiles with no harm to humans. But when it fails to intercept , people on the protected side get hurt.

Move to the offensive side of the spectrum, and the picture changes immediately. Project Maven, launched by the U.S. Department of Defense in 2017, was designed to use AI to process drone surveillance footage and identify objects of military interest, vehicles, weapons, and patterns of movement, the things that analysts were spending thousands of hours reviewing manually. The project created significant controversy inside Google, which was initially a contractor, when employees learned their work was being used for military targeting applications. Google eventually withdrew. The Pentagon continued with other partners.

The core function of Project Maven is intelligence analysis: making sense of enormous volumes of visual data faster than human teams can. That is useful and relatively uncontroversial as military AI applications go. The controversy arises when you trace the chain from "AI identifies a target" to "what happens next," because the chain does not stop at identification. A target identified is a target that someone or something will eventually act on.

Palantir Technologies has military contracts with the U.S. and allied governments for data integration and battlefield-intelligence platforms. Its systems pull together data from multiple sensors, signals intelligence, human reporting, and satellite imagery, and present it in a unified operational picture that commanders can use to make decisions faster and with more confidence. Again, human-in-the-loop in principle. But "faster and with more confidence" has its own implications, because speed and confidence can reduce the time and inclination for deliberation, which is the good kind of friction that sometimes prevents bad decisions.

In Ukraine, AI has been used by both sides in various capacities, from drone navigation to artillery targeting assistance to the analysis of satellite imagery for battlefield assessment. The war in Ukraine has functioned, among other things, as a live laboratory for military AI applications at a scale and intensity that no peacetime exercise could replicate. The lessons being absorbed by militaries around the world will shape war doctrine decisions for the next generation.

China has been explicit in its ambitions for military AI. Its People's Liberation Army has stated goals for AI integration across command, control, and weapons systems, with a target timeline that suggests they are not treating this as a distant aspiration.

Russia has pursued autonomous weapons development, including an unmanned ground combat vehicle, which has been tested in Syria.

South Korea has deployed autonomous sentry guns along the demilitarized zone with North Korea, systems that can detect and engage targets without a human trigger in certain modes.

The new arms race is on. That is not an opinion. It is a description of what is happening.

The Anthropic moment

The U.S. Department of Defense approached Anthropic, the company that makes the Claude AI system, about deploying Claude in a military context. The Department wanted the ability to run Claude in a fully autonomous mode for certain wartime decision-making applications. It wanted human-out-of-the loop functionality. Anthropic said no.

A major AI company turned down a government contract because it concluded that a human-out-of-the-loop scenario for warfare decisions was untested and, responsibly enabling it, too dangerous. In an industry that is not exactly famous for saying no to large contracts, this was a meaningful line in the sand.

Anthropic's reasoning was not complicated. An AI system acting autonomously in a warfare context, making decisions without human review, creates a chain of accountability that leads nowhere. When the AI directs a missile strike on a location it assessed as an enemy compound and the location turns out to be a school, who answers for that? The engineers who wrote the code? The generals who deployed the system? The procurement officers who signed the contract? The algorithm itself, which cannot be court-martialed, tried for war crimes, or held accountable in any legal framework that currently exists?

The absence of accountability is a feature of autonomous military AI. The entire point of removing humans from the loop is to act faster than human decision cycles allow. But human decision cycles are also where accountability lives.

You cannot have both the speed of autonomous action and the accountability of human judgment.

The choice to remove humans from the loop is also a choice to remove the moral and legal architecture that warfare, for all its horror, has spent centuries trying to construct.

The laws of armed conflict, codified in the Geneva Conventions and developed through decades of international law, assume human judgment. They assume a person is involved who can distinguish a combatant from a civilian, who can assess proportionality, and who can weigh military necessity against humanitarian consequences. An algorithm can be programmed with rules. It cannot exercise judgment in the way those rules require. The gap between following a rule and understanding why the rule exists is the gap that gets people killed when the rule meets a situation its drafters did not anticipate.

Assessing AI at war

It would be a mistake to take all of this and conclude that AI has no place in military applications. It clearly does, and the question is not whether, but where and under what constraints. AI is good at processing information at a scale and speed that no human team can match. The volume of data generated by a modern military operation, satellite imagery, signals intercepts, drone feeds, weather data, logistics tracking, enemy communications, and terrain analysis, is simply beyond what human analysts can meaningfully process in real time. AI can synthesize this information, identify patterns, and present commanders with a cleaner operational picture than they would otherwise have. That helps. It is also, if done right, human-in-the-loop: the AI informs, the human decides.

AI is good at logistics. Supply chains in military operations are complex, and the consequences of failure, such as troops without ammunition, fuel that does not arrive, or medical supplies delayed, are severe. Optimizing those chains with AI, predicting demand, routing supplies, and anticipating bottlenecks, is an application where the risk of error is manageable and the benefit is real.

AI is useful in cybersecurity and cyber operations, both offensive and defensive. The speed at which cyberattacks move and the volume of network traffic that needs to be analyzed for intrusion detection are both well beyond human capacity without machine assistance. This is an area where AI has been deployed for years and where the debate about human oversight is somewhat less fraught, because the consequences, while serious, are not measured in immediate physical casualties.

AI earns its keep in war-gaming and simulations. The ability to run thousands of battlefield scenarios, test different strategies against different adversaries' responses, and develop policy based on simulated outcomes rather than real ones has obvious value. Computers have been used for this for decades. AI makes the simulations dramatically more sophisticated. The *War Games* movies are for real.

Where AI should not be operating autonomously is in the direct application of lethal force. Not because the technology will never be capable of making those decisions quickly and accurately. It already can in narrow and well-defined situations. But because the decision to take a human life in a military context carries moral, legal, and political weight that cannot be delegated to a machine without consequences that extend far beyond the immediacy of taking a hill.

The moment a country deploys fully autonomous lethal weapons, it has made a statement to every other country in the world: our weapons will act without human review, at machine speed, with no pause for deliberation. The response to that statement, from adversaries who must now plan against a threat that operates faster than any human decision cycle, is to deploy their own autonomous systems or to find ways to deceive, spoof, or hack the ones they are facing.

The escalation dynamics of autonomous weapons are not well understood, and they are not being adequately studied before autonomous systems are deployed.

The Arms Race Nobody Voted For

The new arms race is not about nuclear warheads or aircraft carrier tonnage. It is about which country can most effectively embed AI into its military decision-making and operational capabilities. This race has some features of the nuclear arms race that Petrov nearly became a casualty of, and some features that are new and arguably more dangerous.

Like nuclear weapons, military AI creates pressure for first-mover advantage. If your adversary's autonomous systems can identify and engage targets faster than your human commanders can authorize a response, you are at a disadvantage. That pressure pushes toward delegation: give the machines more authority, reduce the human-in-the-loop, move toward the out-of-the-loop model because speed wins. This logic is self-reinforcing in the way that nuclear arms competition was self-reinforcing. Each country's decision to escalate becomes the justification for every other country's decision to escalate.

Unlike nuclear weapons, military AI does not come with the same clarity of consequence. You can explain to a politician or a general what a nuclear exchange looks like. Images from the Hiroshima and Nagasaki atomic-bomb detonations are available. The straightforward concept of mutually assured destruction served as a deterrent for decades. The risks of autonomous military AI systems are less visual, more technical, and more abstract, which makes them harder to build political will around and easier to ignore until something goes catastrophically wrong.

There is also a proliferation problem. Nuclear weapons are hard to build. The barriers of physics, engineering, materials, and resources limited the nuclear club to a handful of countries for most of the Cold War. Military AI does not have the same barriers. The underlying technology is developed by commercial companies, is available globally, and is advancing at a pace that outstrips any regulatory framework trying to contain it. A non-state actor with sufficient technical capability and resources can build AI-augmented weapons systems. A smaller country with a good software team and commercial AI tools can potentially punch above its weight in ways that nuclear technology never permitted.

The combination of these factors, the speed pressure, the reduced visibility of risk, and the low barrier to proliferation, makes the AI arms race more dangerous in some respects than the nuclear one, even though the immediate potential for destruction is different in kind.

Who is accountable?

Let's return to the question that Anthropic was clear-eyed enough to raise when it declined the Defense Department's request. When an autonomous AI system makes a lethal error in a military context, the question of accountability is not rhetorical. It is the load-bearing question for the entire legal and ethical framework of warfare. And it does not currently have a satisfying answer.

The software developer who wrote the targeting algorithm did not order the strike. The general who deployed the system made a policy decision, not an operational one. The government that procured the system is a political institution, not a moral agent in the legal sense. The algorithm itself cannot be charged, sanctioned, or made to face consequences.

In conventional warfare, there is a human somewhere in the loop who fired the weapon. That human can be investigated, tried, convicted, or exonerated. The process is imperfect and many times inadequate, but it exists. It creates accountability, which creates at least some deterrent against abuse. When you take humans out of the equation, you also take away the method that ensures warfare, however imperfectly, adheres to legal and ethical norms.

The International Committee of the Red Cross has called for legal rules specifically prohibiting autonomous weapons from being used against people, meaning that any use of force against a human target should require human control and judgment. As of this writing, no binding international agreement to this effect exists. The debate is ongoing, and the weapons are already being deployed.

Last man standing

There is a thought that I keep coming back to when thinking about military AI, and it is one that cuts through a lot of the abstraction. Whichever country can most effectively embed AI into its military capabilities will have a decisive advantage in any large-scale conflict. That is the competitive reality under which every major military power is operating. Ignore it, and you'll lose. Embrace it without adequate safeguards and you risk something that is harder to name but potentially worse.

The Petrov scenario is the cleanest illustration of what adequate safeguards mean in practice. The value Petrov provided in 1983 was not technical. It was human. It was the ability to recognize that something that looked like the threshold for catastrophic action did not feel strategically coherent, and to sit with that unease long enough to avoid triggering the end of the world. An AI system operating at machine speed with a protocol for certain inputs has no equivalent capacity. It does not wonder whether five missiles make sense. It counts five missiles and executes. End of the world.

Human-in-the-loop is an ethical requirement, not something that smarter AI can engineer away, and it reflects something about what it means for lethal force to be used. That keeping humans-in-the-loop makes autonomous systems slower is important, and some would say, necessary.

The countries that figure out how to use AI to fortify human military judgment, rather than to replace it, will be in a better position than the ones that treat the goal as removing human judgment from the equation entirely. Not because the first approach is tactically superior in every scenario. Because the second approach creates risks of escalation, of catastrophic error, and of accountability collapse, which are not understood and are not being managed.

We built nuclear weapons before we built the political infrastructure to contain them. We nearly paid for that sequencing multiple times during the Cold War. Stanislav Petrov saved us once that we know of. We should not be designing systems that depend on finding a Stanislav Petrov every time.

11. AI in the Cockpit

There are roughly 45,000 flights in the sky over the United States on any given day. Each one needs to be separated from every other, routed through crowded corridors of airspace, sequenced for landing at airports that have three runways and forty planes trying to use them, and kept away from weather systems that are moving and changing in real time.

A single air traffic controller at a busy facility might be managing fifteen to twenty aircraft simultaneously, making decisions every few seconds, talking on the radio, watching radar, and coordinating with adjacent sectors.

The complexity is staggering. And yet commercial aviation is, statistically, the safest form of long-distance transportation ever devised. You are orders of magnitude more likely to be seriously injured driving to the airport than flying out of it.

Keeping humans in charge of everything did not build that safety record. A careful, decades-long partnership between human judgment and increasingly sophisticated automation built it. Understanding how that partnership works, where it succeeds, where it fails, and where it is heading, tells you something important about where AI belongs in high-stakes systems, and where it does not.

What AI is doing now at 35,000 feet

If you have flown commercially in the last thirty years, you have already trusted your life to AI; you just did not think of it that way.

The autopilot system on a modern commercial aircraft manages altitude, heading, and speed with a precision that no human hand can match over a long flight. The Flight Management System computes the optimal route, calculates fuel burn, sequences the descent, and guides the aircraft to within a few feet of the runway centerline.

The Traffic Collision Avoidance System, known as TCAS, monitors every nearby aircraft independently of air traffic control and issues direct commands to the pilots, climb now or descend now, when it detects a conflict that the humans have not resolved fast enough. Ground proximity warning systems alert crews to terrain that radar has not caught. Weather detection systems paint the sky in real time.

None of this is new. The automation in a modern airliner has been accumulating and improving since the 1960s, and it is remarkable. These systems handle a ton of data, never get fatigued, never get distracted by a conversation in the cockpit, and execute their functions with a consistency that human performance cannot match over a twelve-hour transoceanic flight.

On the ground, AI tools already assist controllers with traffic-flow optimization and workload management. These systems incorporate AI that flags potential aircraft separation issues several minutes before they become emergencies. The AI gives human controllers more time to think and fewer surprises to react to. That is human-in-the-loop working as intended: the machine handles the data processing, and the human handles the judgment.

The question is what happens when you try to push that further.

The Edge Case is the Whole Job

On January 15, 2009, US Airways Flight 1549 took off from LaGuardia Airport in New York and flew directly into a flock of Canada geese at approximately 2,800 feet. Both engines swallowed birds and lost engine power within seconds. The aircraft went from a routine departure to an overweight glider in a blink of an eye.

Captain Chesley "Sully" Sullenberger, with forty years of experience, had roughly three minutes to make a series of decisions for which the entire aviation system had not prepared a specific protocol. The Flight Management System and the automated emergency checklists directed him toward Teterboro Airport in New Jersey.

Every procedural algorithm said: get to a runway. Sully looked at the altitude he was losing, the distance to Teterboro, and concluded he could not make it. He chose to land in the Hudson River. The lesser of two evils.

He was right. All 155 people on board survived. Sully was initially scrutinized by the FAA, which ran simulations suggesting a runway landing might have been possible, before those simulations were adjusted to account for the human reaction time that a real emergency involves rather than the instant response a computer model assumes. The hero label eventually stuck.

The reason this story matters for AI is not that Sully was a superhero. It is that the situation he faced had essentially no precedent in the data used to train the AI. In the entire history of commercial aviation, there had not been many incidents involving dual engine failure from bird ingestion while on climb-out over a densely populated urban area with multiple airports within varying ranges of reach. AI systems learn from historical data. When the situation in front of it has no meaningful historical analog, AI has no reliable framework to apply. They are, as Claude put it when I posed this question, like a child seeing a lion at the zoo for the first time. They do not know what they are seeing. This is the essence of an AI "edge case."

Air traffic control faces the same problem at the system level. Controllers handle runway traffic, equipment failures, pilots who stop responding, medical emergencies in the cockpit, and dozens of other scenarios that do not appear in routine operations. For routine operations, a well-designed AI manages the workload better than a human.

It is in the unusual and the unexpected where human reasoning, human improvisation, and the human ability to detect stress or impairment in another person's voice still carry weight that no current AI system can replicate.

This is not a sentimental argument for keeping humans in the loop because of tradition. It is an observation about what AI is and is not good at. The rare event is not a rounding error in aviation safety. It is the entire reason pilots and controllers exist.

When Automation Goes Wrong

The safety record of commercial aviation is impressive. What is less discussed publicly is how many of the serious accidents in the last two decades have involved automation that malfunctioned, misled its crew, or worked exactly as programmed in situations where the programming was wrong.

On June 1, 2009, Air France Flight 447 departed Rio de Janeiro for Paris and flew into a system of thunderstorms over the Atlantic. The autopilot disconnected when ice crystals temporarily blocked a key airspeed sensor. The aircraft entered a stall; the nose pitched up, and the plane fell from 38,000 feet into the ocean. All 228 people on board were killed.

The investigation found something that has haunted aviation safety discussions ever since. The pilots, confronted with a situation they had rarely, if ever, encountered in actual flight, responded incorrectly. They pulled back on the controls when the correct response to a stall is to push forward. They continued pulling back as the stall warnings sounded repeatedly.

For several minutes, trained commercial pilots with thousands of hours between them flew a functional aircraft into the ocean because they had lost the manual flying skills and aerodynamic intuition that would have let them recognize and recover from a stall.

The reason those skills had eroded was automation. In normal operations, commercial pilots hand-fly their aircraft for an average of about three minutes per flight. The rest of the time, the autopilot manages the aircraft. Over years of flying this way, pilots lose the tactile and instinctive familiarity with the aircraft's handling that earlier generations of aviators built through thousands of hours of manual flight.

When the automation disconnects in a crisis and hands control back to a human, what they get back is not always a skilled manual pilot. Sometimes it is someone who has not truly hand-flown an aircraft under pressure in years.

The Air France 447 accident was not a story about automation failing. It was a story about automation succeeding so well for so long that the humans it was supporting forgot how to do the job without it.

737 MAX: When AI is the problem

If Air France 447 illustrates what happens when pilots can no longer handle the airplane without AI, the Boeing 737 MAX crashes illustrate what happens when the AI itself is the hazard.

In October 2018, Lion Air Flight 610 crashed into the Java Sea shortly after takeoff from Jakarta. All 189 people on board were killed. Five months later, Ethiopian Airlines Flight 302 crashed in nearly identical circumstances, killing all 157 on board. Both aircraft were new Boeing 737 MAX jets. Both accidents were caused by the same system.

Boeing had added a flight control system called MCAS, the Maneuvering Characteristics Augmentation System, to the 737 MAX to compensate for handling changes introduced by a new, heavier engine design. MCAS was designed to push the nose of the aircraft down automatically if a sensor showed the plane was pitching up too steeply. The problem was that MCAS relied on a single sensor, and when that sensor gave an erroneous reading, MCAS activated repeatedly, pushing the nose down, resisting the pilots' attempts to pull it back up, and ultimately driving both aircraft into the ground.

In the Lion Air accident, the flight crew fought the system for most of the flight before losing control. In the Ethiopian accident, the crew followed the Boeing emergency procedure exactly as trained, but the procedure was inadequate for the intensity of the MCAS activation they faced. The aircraft could not be recovered.

The 737 MAX crashes killed 346 people, grounded the entire global fleet for twenty months, cost Boeing tens of billions of dollars, and triggered one of the most consequential aviation safety investigations in history. They also produced a finding that applies directly to any conversation about AI in high-stakes systems: when automation is given authority over a critical function and that automation has a flaw, the humans who are theoretically in control may not have enough time, information, or trained response to overcome it.

The pilots on both flights knew something was wrong. They fought the system. They lost. Not because they were incompetent, but because the system had authority it should not have had without better safeguards, better pilot training, and more transparency about what it was doing and why.

The skill erosion problem

The research on pilot skill degradation due to automation dependence has been building for years, and it makes for disturbing reading. Studies have found that pilots who fly highly automated aircraft show measurably degraded manual flying skills compared with pilots of earlier generations.

The concern is not theoretical. Aviation safety regulators on multiple continents have issued recommendations about it.

The phenomenon has a name in human factors research: automation complacency. It describes the tendency of humans who work with highly reliable automated systems to reduce their active monitoring of what the system is doing, to trust its outputs without verification, and to lose the proficiency that comes only from regularly performing a task yourself. When the system works correctly, complacency is invisible. When the system fails, it can be catastrophic.

The 2009 Colgan Air crash near Buffalo, New York, offers another illustration. The first officer on that flight had apparently not been adequately trained to recognize and respond to a "stick shaker," which is the control column vibration that warns of an approaching stall. When it activated, the captain responded by pulling back on the controls rather than pushing forward, which is the instinctive but wrong response. The plane stalled and crashed, killing all 49 people on board and one person on the ground.

Post-accident investigation revealed significant questions about training standards, fatigue, and the degree to which the pilots understood the aircraft's behavior in unusual situations.

In each of these cases, a thread runs through the story. The automation handled the routine flying. The humans had limited recent experience with the non-routine. When the non-routine arrived, the gap in proficiency showed at the worst possible moment.

This is not unique to aviation. It is the automation paradox: the more reliable the system, the less practice humans get handling failures, which means the worse they perform when failures occur. In aviation, where the margin for error during certain phases of flight is measured in seconds, that paradox has consequences.

Human-in-loop to human-on-loop

Aviation is already moving from the first model of human-AI collaboration toward the second, and the FAA controller shortage is hastening the transition.

In the human-in-the-loop model, the AI recommends and humans approve every significant decision. Controllers are actively managing each aircraft with AI tools supporting them. Pilots set their automatics but are expected to be capable of hand-flying the aircraft at any time.

In the human-on-the-loop model, AI manages routine operations autonomously and humans supervise, ready to intervene when the situation exceeds what automation can handle. Controllers manage larger geographic sectors with AI handling the routine aircraft-separation math and alerting humans to conflicts. Pilots fly highly automated aircraft with fewer manual intervention requirements, focusing more on system monitoring and decision-making than on direct aircraft control.

The trajectory is clear. The question is whether the transition is being managed well, and whether the humans who are increasingly relegated to supervisory roles are being trained and maintained at a level that makes their intervention meaningful when it is needed.

Because the intervention will be needed. The edge cases will come. The bird strikes, the sensor failures, the incapacitated pilots, the simultaneous equipment failures, and the situations that no algorithm was trained to handle. And when they come, the human in that supervisory seat had better be more than someone who knows how to watch a screen.

My assessment

AI belongs in aviation. It is already there; it has made aviation safer, and it will expand its role significantly over the coming decades. The FAA controller shortage will be partially addressed by AI absorbing more of the routine workload. Cockpit automation will continue to improve. Autonomous cargo aircraft will probably become operational before autonomous passenger aircraft. The proliferation of AI in travel is not in doubt.

What is also not in doubt, if you pay attention to the accident record, is that the partnership between human and machine in aviation requires careful management that does not always receive it. Automation that erodes manual skill, automation that has design flaws, automation that operates without adequate transparency, and automation that is given authority without adequate safeguards. All these have contributed to crashes that killed people.

The lesson is not that automation is dangerous. It is that human-machine collaboration requires sustained, deliberate investment in keeping the human half of that partnership competent and engaged. You cannot hand more authority to automation and simultaneously reduce the training and involvement of the humans who are supposed to catch what the automation misses.

Sully saved 155 lives because he had forty years of experience and the judgment (and courage) to override the algorithm. The question that aviation safety researchers are asking is whether the next Sully will have what it takes to do the same thing, or whether decades of automation have changed what it means to be a pilot in ways that make that kind of judgment harder to find when it is needed most.

12. AI in Medicine

You felt that crunching sound in your knee trying to be cool playing pickup basketball. Maybe you went for a shot you had no business going for. Now you are in the emergency room, your knee is swollen, and the medical team has sent you for an X-ray before anyone has even asked whether you have insurance.

The radiologist who reads that image is experienced. She has been doing this for thirty years. Over a thirty-year career, reading several hundred knee images a year, she will have reviewed perhaps ten thousand knee X-rays. That sounds like a lot.

Now, consider the AI.

In the US, more than three million knee injuries show up in emergency rooms every year. The AI read all of them. This year. Last year too. And the year before. You are not looking at ten thousand knee images. You are looking at thirty million and counting. The AI has seen every unusual presentation, every rare fracture pattern, every subtle sign of early arthritis that a tired radiologist at the end of a night shift might miss. When the AI looks at your knee, it is drawing on a library of experience that no human being could accumulate in a hundred lifetimes.

This is where AI is most powerful in medicine, and the principle holds across every application we will discuss in this chapter. When a task involves consuming volumes of data, identifying patterns, and flagging anomalies, the machine wins. Not because it is smarter than a doctor. Because scale is a form of expertise, and the machine has scale that no human can touch.

Why radiology went first

Radiology was the first major medical specialty to be transformed by AI, and the reason is straightforward. Follow the data.

A radiological image is, at its core, a structured dataset. Every pixel has a value. Every scan follows a standardized format. The images are labeled with diagnoses and patient outcomes. You have volumes of structured, labeled data, and you have a task; identify what is normal and what is not. This is a pattern-recognition problem. That is the environment where machine learning performs best.

The results have been striking. AI systems are now standard tools for flagging anomalies in mammograms, chest X-rays, and brain scans. In diabetic retinopathy screening, AI has achieved accuracy in the high nineties for catching early signs of the disease in retinal images, often identifying minute vessel changes before a human reviewer sees them. Google's system, developed with ophthalmologists and validated across tens of thousands of cases, has been deployed in parts of the world where there are simply not enough trained ophthalmologists to screen every diabetic patient at risk. The AI does not replace the specialist. It extends the reach of specialist-level screening to places and populations that would otherwise go unscreened.

Diabetic retinopathy is the leading cause of preventable blindness in working-age adults. Caught early, it is treatable. Caught late, it is not. The gap between those two outcomes is where AI is filling a real need as a deployed clinical tool doing work right now.

The same pattern is playing out in pathology, where AI systems analyze tissue samples for cancer cells with a consistency that does not fatigue at slide number three hundred, and in dermatology, where AI models trained on hundreds of thousands of labeled skin images can flag suspicious lesions for physician review with accuracy that matches board-certified dermatologists in controlled studies. The common thread in all of it is the same: large, structured, labeled datasets, combined with a well-defined pattern-recognition task.

Sepsis: when fast beats smart

When your body is overwhelmed by infection and its immune system cannot fight back fast enough, the condition is called sepsis. It is responsible for roughly twenty percent of all deaths worldwide. If that number surprises you, you are not alone. Sepsis does not get the public attention that cancer or heart disease does, but by mortality statistics, it belongs in the same conversation.

The clinical challenge with sepsis is timing. The earlier it is identified, the better the patient's odds. But sepsis does not announce itself clearly in its early stages. It builds. The vital signs shift gradually, the lab values drift in ways that are easy to attribute to other causes, and by the time the picture is unambiguous, significant damage may already have been done. Physicians working a busy hospital floor are monitoring multiple patients simultaneously, reviewing data that arrives at different times in different forms, and making judgment calls about which changes are significant and which are noise.

AI is better at this specific task than a human clinician working in real time. Not because the AI is more knowledgeable about sepsis, but because it can simultaneously monitor every data point across every patient, compare those patterns against millions of historical cases, and flag early warning signs that no individual clinician could reliably catch while also managing everything else on the ward.

The key phrase is "aggregate and analyze in real time." A nurse reviewing a patient at the start of a shift sees a snapshot. The AI sees a continuous movie running across every data stream simultaneously, drawing a line through the trend rather than evaluating each point in isolation. Early sepsis warning systems deployed in hospitals have measurably reduced mortality rates by compressing the time between the first detectable signs of deterioration and clinical intervention. That compressed timeline, measured in hours, is the difference between successful treatment and late-stage crisis management.

Drug discovery

The pharmaceutical industry has used AI to reduce drug discovery timelines that historically ran to ten or fifteen years. This is not yet delivering finished medications to pharmacy shelves at a dramatically faster rate, because clinical trials still take time and regulatory approval still requires the evidence. But the early-stage work, identifying drug candidates, predicting side effects, and ruling out dead ends, is being done faster and with more precision than was possible a decade ago. The first drugs designed substantially with AI assistance are now in clinical trials.

Personalized medicine is the further horizon. AI can analyze a patient's entire genome and identify mutations that drive their specific cancer, then match those mutations against the catalog of existing targeted therapies or flag candidates for new ones. The concept of a treatment designed for a single patient's specific biology, once the stuff of science fiction, is becoming operationally real in disciplines like oncology.

Surgeons are beginning to use virtual three-dimensional models of a specific patient's organ built from imaging data, to simulate complex procedures before making the first incision. The simulation catches complications that would otherwise emerge unexpectedly in the operating room.

The AI application that doctors love

There is an application of AI in medicine that does not appear in headlines about fancy treatments or big diagnostic wins. It may be the one that has the most immediate impact on the quality of care most patients receive.

Doctors in the US spend an extraordinary portion of their working hours on documentation. By some estimates, for every hour a physician spends with a patient, they spend two hours on administrative tasks: entering notes into the electronic health record, handling prior authorizations, managing referrals, and dealing with billing codes. This is not what most people went to medical school to do. It is a driver of physician burnout, which is itself a significant contributor to the physician shortage that strains the healthcare system.

AI ambient scribing tools listen to the conversation between a doctor and patient, understand the clinical content of that conversation, and automatically generate a structured note in the electronic health record. The physician reviews and approves it, but the forty-five minutes of post-visit documentation is reduced to a few minutes of editing. The physician can look at the patient during the appointment rather than at a keyboard. The visit becomes, by multiple accounts from physicians using these tools, more human.

Workflow optimization is the less visible companion to ambient scribing. AI systems that predict patient discharge dates, model hospital bed availability, and flag patients at risk of readmission are reducing the administrative friction that clogs emergency rooms and extends hospital stays. These are not glamorous applications. They do not cure diseases. But they free up resources, reduce wait times, and improve the environment in which clinical care is delivered. In a healthcare system under significant strain, that matters.

Ethical Problems

AI in medicine has a bias problem, and it runs deeper than most people realize.

AI systems learn from the data they are trained on. If that data is not representative of the population the system will be used on, the system will not perform equally well across that population. This is not a hypothetical concern. It is a documented reality.

Consider the knee imaging example. If the thirty million knee images that trained the AI were drawn disproportionately from white male patients between twenty and fifty years old in urban academic medical centers, then the AI's expertise is concentrated in that demographic. A seventy-year-old woman, a teenager with a different skeletal structure, a patient with a prior injury that altered the anatomy of the joint: these are the edge cases.

The AI has seen fewer of them. The AI's confidence on your scan may not be warranted because your presentation differs from the core of its training data.

The path toward correction is not simple. You cannot solve a data representation problem by adjusting the algorithm after the fact. Fix the training data, which means ensuring that the populations underrepresented in historical medical datasets are adequately represented in the data used to train future systems. This requires deliberate effort, ongoing monitoring, and a level of statistical rigor in the construction of training sets that has not always been applied. The AI models that will eventually serve diverse populations well are not here yet.

The black box

The second major ethical problem is the black box. Many of the most accurate AI diagnostic systems cannot explain their reasoning in terms that a physician can evaluate or a patient can understand. The model looks at your scan, weights several hundred variables in ways that cannot be articulated in human language, and produces a probability estimate. The number might be accurate. The reasoning behind it is opaque.

This creates a clinical dilemma. A physician is ethically obligated to obtain informed consent before a significant medical decision: surgery, a course of chemotherapy, or a procedure with meaningful risk. Informed consent requires explanation. If the recommendation is based on an AI's assessment and neither the physician nor the AI can explain why that assessment was reached, the informed consent conversation becomes difficult to conduct honestly.

There is also the issue of physician trust. Most clinicians are trained to be skeptical of conclusions they cannot follow logically. An AI recommendation that emerges from a process they cannot interrogate or verify puts them in the position of either accepting it on faith or overriding it based on their own judgment, with no clear framework for deciding which is appropriate.

Who is accountable?

When an AI-assisted diagnosis misses a tumor and the patient's cancer is caught a year later at a more advanced stage, who is responsible?

The honest answer in 2026 is that no one is entirely sure, and the legal frameworks have not caught up to the technology. The physician who ordered the AI tool and acted on its output carries clinical responsibility for the care decision but did not design the algorithm or control its training data. Various legal disclaimers protect the company that built and sold the tool.

This gap in accountability is not a minor administrative concern. It shapes how physicians use these tools, how aggressively companies validate them for diverse populations, and how much transparency is provided to patients about when and how AI is involved in their care. Patients often do not know that an AI system played a role in evaluating their imaging or assessing their risk. Whether they have a right to know, and whether they have a right to opt out, are questions that regulators in most countries have not yet answered definitively.

The liability ambiguity also creates perverse incentives. A physician who follows an AI recommendation and gets a bad outcome is in a legally uncertain position. A physician who overrides an AI recommendation and gets a bad outcome may be in a worse one, because they deviated from the tool's guidance. Neither of those incentive structures produces good medicine.

Skills erosion

There is a concern among veteran physicians that gets less attention than the headline breakthroughs, but that deserves serious consideration.

Younger doctors entering medicine today do so in an environment where AI handles a significant portion of the initial diagnostic workload. They train alongside these tools from the beginning. The AI flags the anomaly; they evaluate the flag. Over years of practice, the direct pattern recognition skills that earlier generations of clinicians built through unassisted diagnosis may develop more slowly, or not at all.

This is the same conundrum seen in aviation. The more reliable and capable the automation, the less frequently the human practitioner exercises the underlying skill, and the more that skill atrophies. In medicine, the consequence of atrophied clinical intuition is not theoretical. It is the physician who cannot function effectively when the AI fails, the power goes out, the system is unavailable for maintenance, or the patient presents with something so unusual that the AI has no useful prior reference.

Experienced clinicians describe something they call "clinical gestalt," the integration of hundreds of subtle observations into an overall sense of how sick a patient is, independent of any single data point. A patient who looks wrong in a way that the chart does not fully capture. The quality of distress in someone's face. The way a patient answers a question. These observations are difficult to quantify and impossible to input into a model, and they are built through thousands of hours of face-to-face clinical experience.

If the next generation of physicians develops that experience primarily in partnership with AI assistance, medicine gets a tool it has not fully accounted for: a workforce with strong skills in AI-assisted diagnosis and potentially weaker skills in diagnosis without assistance. Whether that trade-off is acceptable depends heavily on how reliable the AI assistance turns out to be when it matters most.

Data privacy

AI requires data. And a lot of it. The training sets for medical AI systems are built from patient records, imaging studies, lab results, and clinical notes collected from healthcare systems over years or decades. That data is nominally anonymized before it is used, meaning names and direct identifiers are stripped out.

The problem is that anonymization is less reliable than it sounds. Researchers have demonstrated repeatedly that AI systems can re-identify patients by cross-referencing multiple data sources, matching patterns in supposedly anonymous records against other available information. A birth date, a zip code, a rare diagnosis, and a specific procedure date can together identify a unique individual even without a name attached.

The implications are significant. Insurance companies with access to re-identified medical data could use it to adjust premiums or deny coverage. Employers with access could make hiring decisions. Pharmaceutical companies could target individuals with specific conditions for marketing. None of these uses are authorized under the consent patients give when they receive medical care, and the technical barriers to preventing them are not as solid as the regulatory frameworks assume.

A conclusion

AI in medicine is already here. It is reading imaging studies, flagging deteriorating patients, designing drug candidates, and listening to heartbeats.

The ethical problems are real, and they are not fully solved. Algorithmic bias, the black box, accountability gaps, skills atrophy, and data privacy concerns are documented, observed, and in some cases already causing harm. The responsible use of AI in medicine requires addressing these concerns seriously and continuously.

The framework that makes most sense, and that the AI engines I consulted both arrived at independently, is the same framework that applies to autonomous vehicles and to warfare. AI should be augmenting human judgment, not replacing it. The physician remains responsible. The AI extends her capability, reduces her administrative burden, and catches things she might otherwise miss.

The human-in-the-loop is not a temporary concession to current limitations. It is the right architecture for a domain where the stakes of errors are measured in human lives.

You know how they say it is good to get a second opinion on a serious medical issue? The next time you are sitting in the exam room waiting for results, it is entirely reasonable to ask whether an AI has reviewed your imaging. In a growing number of hospitals, the answer is yes, and that is a good thing. The AI brought thirty million knee images to the conversation. Your doctor brought clinical judgment, the ability to look you in the eye, and the accountability that comes with a medical license.

You need both.

CONCLUSION

I visualize a time when we will be to robots what dogs are to humans, and I'm rooting for the machines.

~Claude Shannon, the father of information theory, which is the basis for all computing and AI.

What you now know

You made it. That either means you are a dedicated reader, or you skipped straight to the end to see how it turns out. Either way, congratulations.

No Adult Left Behind draws on the purpose of the No Child Left Behind Act of 2001, which installed federal standards for education of children. If your school was not teaching the right things and students' standardized test scores were not improving, your school received less federal funding. The program was controversial, but the awareness of the problem it created was real.

The purpose of the book title is to draw attention to the fact that adults need to go back to school and learn how to use AI in everyday life. It is not a heavy lift, and this book is trying to give you a nudge.

Adults who do not get with the AI program will "age" faster than their peers who embrace AI. Non-AI users will be left out of future cocktail party (and career) conversations, because they never took advantage of having all the world's knowledge in the palm of their hand.

But before you close the book, let's talk about what we learned, because the common threads running through these chapters are more useful than any individual story about a knee X-ray or a stock pick or Canadian geese that almost brought down a plane.

The data thread

Every topic in this book, from radiology to autonomous driving to the AI that screens your resume before a human ever reads it, rests on the same foundation. Scale.

The AI reading your knee X-ray is not smarter than your radiologist. It has seen more knee X-rays than your radiologist could review in a hundred lifetimes. The AI flagging sepsis in hospitalized patients is not more knowledgeable about infection than an intensivist with thirty years of experience. It is monitoring more patients, more data streams, and more historical patterns simultaneously than any human clinician could manage while also doing everything else their job requires.

This matters because scale is a form of expertise for which we do not have a good human equivalent.

The flip side of this is the thing that creates problems. AI trained on data that does not represent you does not work as well for you. The 2019 study that found a commercial algorithm recommending less care for Black patients was not a glitch. It was an accurate reflection of the dataset it was trained on, which itself was a reflection of decades of unequal care. The AI was just efficient about identifying the pattern.

This is true in hiring too. An AI screening resumes is only as unbiased as the historical hiring decisions it learned from. If the company historically hired a certain kind of person, with a certain type of education and background, the model will look for that certain kind of person, regardless of whether that pattern ever made sense. Scale amplifies whatever was in the data, the good and the bad, with equal enthusiasm.

When you use AI, the right question is not just "Is this accurate?" The right question is "What was this trained on, and is it relevant to me?"

The edge case thread

Here is the thread that runs through aviation, medicine, warfare, autonomous vehicles, and the *Titanic*. The AI handles the routine case with a competence that no human can match. And then the unusual thing happens.

Captain Sullenberger lost both engines over Manhattan at 2,800 feet. Every procedural algorithm pointed toward Teterboro Airport. Sully looked at the numbers, looked at the altitude he was losing, and chose the Hudson River. Every algorithm was wrong. He was right.

The Boeing 737 MAX's MCAS system worked exactly as programmed. The problem was that it was programmed to trust a single sensor, and when that sensor failed, the automation had more authority over the aircraft than the pilots trying to override it. Three hundred and forty-six people died because the edge case, a single sensor giving an erroneous reading, was not accounted for in a system that had been given enormous authority.

The *Titanic* received seven ice warnings in the hours before it hit the iceberg. The data and the pattern were there. No single person was aggregating all of it simultaneously and asking what it meant collectively. The ship was moving at near-full speed into an ice field it had been warned about repeatedly, and nobody in a position to slow it down had been handed all seven warnings at once.

These are not stories about technology failing. They are stories about what happens at the boundaries of what any system, human or artificial, was designed to handle. AI crushes it in the scenario it has seen before. It is often dangerously unprepared for the scenario it has not. The edge case is not a rounding error. It is the entire reason experienced human judgment still has value in high-stakes systems.

This is the part of the book I want you to remember most, because it applies whether you are thinking about AI tools in your job, in medicine, in the cockpit, or in a weapons system. When someone tells you that AI has achieved human-level performance on a benchmark, the correct follow-up question is: what happens when the situation is nothing like the benchmark?

The loop thread

The framework that kept appearing in chapter after chapter, human-in-the-loop, human-on-the-loop, human-out-of-the-loop, is not just an abstraction for aviation safety researchers and military ethicists. It is the organizing principle for thinking about every AI deployment you will encounter in your professional life.

Human-in-the-loop means the AI recommends and a human approves every significant decision. This is the AI that drafts the performance review of your subordinate, and you edit it before it goes out. This is the AI radiology tool that flags an anomaly, and a physician confirms it. This is the AI that surfaces job candidates, and a hiring manager still makes the call. The human is in the chain. Every decision touches a person who is accountable for it.

Human-on-the-loop means the AI manages routine operations autonomously while a human supervises and can intervene. Air traffic control is moving in this direction. Hospital workflow optimization is already here. This type of AI handles the routine aircraft separation math, the routine bed assignments, and routine fraud detection. The human watches, monitors, and jumps in when something is outside what the automation can handle. The human is still there. Just less hands-on than before.

Human-out-of-the-loop is where things get a little weird and scary, and it is the configuration that most of us should push back on hardest in the near term. Autonomous weapons that select and engage targets without human approval. Hiring algorithms that reject candidates before a person ever sees the application. Loan approval systems that deny credit based on patterns a human never reviews. When accountability disappears from the chain, the consequences of errors, biases, and edge cases fall on people who had no say in the decision that affected them.

The loop framework is useful because it forces the right question. For any AI application you encounter, ask where the human is. If the answer is "mostly just watching," ask whether the human has the training, the information, and the time to intervene meaningfully when something goes wrong. If the answer is "nowhere," ask who is responsible when it fails.

The prompting thread

This one is less dramatic than edge cases and autonomous weapons, but it is the one with the most immediate practical impact on your daily life.

Throughout this book, we compared what AI produced when asked lazy questions to what it produced when asked well-constructed ones. The difference was not minor. A vague prompt about whether to accept a job offer produces generic platitudes about work-life balance. A prompt that includes your industry, your current compensation, your geographic constraints, your risk tolerance, and three specific things you want the AI to evaluate produces something you can use.

The pattern that emerged from chapter after chapter is that the AI is only as useful as the context you give it. The more specific you are about who you are, what you are trying to accomplish, and what format you want the answer in, the more useful the output. "Garbage in, garbage out" is not just a computer science term. It is the operating principle of every AI tool you will encounter.

And then there is the iteration piece. Sending one prompt and accepting the first answer is the equivalent of asking a colleague a question, hearing their initial response, and treating that as the final word without any follow-up. The value of AI often emerges in the second and third exchanges, when you push back, ask for alternatives, challenge an assumption, or tell it what it missed. The people who are getting the most out of these tools are not the people who ask once and walk away. They are the people who treat it as a conversation.

The ask two AIs thread

This one came up repeatedly in the research for this book, and it is worth naming directly. When I asked Claude and ChatGPT to pick stocks, they came back with meaningfully different portfolios. ChatGPT leaned toward momentum and brand recognition. Claude dug into catalysts and undervalued positions. They were both wrong, for the record, but they were wrong in different and informative ways. When I asked both about AI in medicine, one emphasized clinical efficiency, and the other led with ethical risk. When I asked about autonomous vehicles, the answers diverged on the trolley problem in ways that revealed different underlying software frameworks.

The lesson is not that one AI is better than the other. The lesson is that treating any single AI as the authoritative source on a complex question is the same mistake as reading one analyst's report before making an investment decision or signing up for a complex medical procedure without a second opinion. The value is in the comparison. Where the two AIs agree, you can feel reasonably confident. Where they diverge, you have found the interesting question worth some digging.

This is also a useful check on the AI's relationship to your existing assumptions. If you prompt only one AI and it confirms what you already believed, you have learned nothing. Ask a second one and ask it to provide the opposing view and tell you what you are missing. The best use of these tools is not as an answer machine; it is as a thinking partner who has read more than you have and has no ego invested in being right.

The skill atrophy thread

This is the hidden concern that will show as AI automations become more commonplace. Pilots who fly highly automated aircraft hand-fly for an average of three minutes per flight. The rest of the time, the autopilot is managing the aircraft. Over years, manual flying skills erode. When the automation disconnects in a crisis, the pilot who takes control is not always a skilled manual aviator. Sometimes it is someone who has not hand-flown an aircraft under pressure in years.

Physicians who train alongside AI diagnostic tools may develop strong skills at evaluating AI recommendations and weaker skills at pattern recognition without AI assistance. Teachers who use AI to draft lesson plans, lawyers who use it to draft briefs, analysts who use it to produce first-draft reports: all of them face the same underlying question. What happens to the underlying skill when the tool is unavailable, or wrong, or operating in a situation it was never trained to handle?

This is not an argument against using the tools. It is an argument for using them in a way that does not hollow out the expertise underneath. Use AI to do more. Be careful about using AI as a substitute for thinking.

My assessment

Here is what I know after thousands of hours conversing with the AIs and having them challenge my thinking. AI is a tool with a specific and well-defined set of strengths, a specific and well-documented set of weaknesses, and a set of ethical complications that the people deploying it have not yet fully worked through.

Your job is to understand enough about both sides of that ledger to use the tool well and to push back when it is being used badly.

The common thread underneath every chapter in this book is human judgment. Not as a sentimental attachment to the way things used to be and not as a refusal to acknowledge what AI can do. But as a requirement for any high-stakes system that operates in a world full of edge cases, biased data, accountability gaps, and situations no algorithm was trained to handle.

You need to know how to prompt. You need to know when to iterate. You need to know when to ask a second AI. You need to know when to override the tool entirely and trust your own judgment, because the confidence of an AI output is not the same thing as the accuracy of it.

You are, whether you have asked to be or not, living in the most significant technological transition since the internet became something ordinary people used to do ordinary things. The people who navigated the internet transition well were the ones who took the extra time to understand the "what" and "how" of a new technology. They were versatile because their understanding of the new technology gave them an advantage over their less-technology literate peers.

Those internet pioneers were, in a word, curious, but also realized that a wave was washing over society and many things would not be the same in the future.

Use what you learned in this book and be curious about AI. You may ask why? Simple answer: don't get left behind.

ACKNOWLEGEMENTS

I have always been a technology enthusiast and in companies I have run, when I have managed teams of highly skilled engineers and software developers, I could not help but admire their methodical thinking and careful approach to problem solving. I tinkered with technologies, but they really built stuff.

Then there was the mini-revolution of no-code app building, followed quickly by the arrival of the big AI models. Suddenly, I could build apps and systems like the geniuses I had admired for so many years. Maybe not as sophisticated (or reliable), but definitely in the category of "cool."

I have been using the big AI models (Gemini, ChatGPT, Grok, and Claude) for some time now and have found them to be loyal companions and, I dare say, articulate. Conversations with the AI models are the basis of the Learning AI series on my blog, theCautionary.com, and for this book.

AI has helped me write this book, but more relevant than being a good editor and a partner that surfaces and debates ideas, AI has forced me to think deeper about problems. Using AI really is different from entering a term into search.

So, my first thank you is to my AI companions that have contributed to me being a better thinker and writer.

Without JD Kleinke, I would never have started down the path as a writer, published my first book, *The Seven Deadly Stupidities*, or my weekly newsletter that I have produced for over 125 weeks in a row. He is an accomplished author, speaker, and always generous with his time.

I am grateful to Guy Kawasaki for his unselfish and practical advice. For those of you who don't know Guy, look him up if you want to see what an incredible career looks like.

Despite his busy schedule, entrepreneur Chris Elbring found the time to offer many relevant comments, some serious, some not, on an early draft.

Seth and Mary Baker have been consistent weekly supporters and a font of ideas for AI topics. Andy and Helen Cappuccino continue to cheer me on enthusiastically. How did I wind up with four lifelong friends that are all doctors that tolerate my attempts being a writer?

Renae and Jay Tesauro provided a thorough markup of a draft from the perspective of a professional author and a technology executive, respectively. And they did it quickly!

My sister-in-law, MaryJo Pierorazio, gets a thank you for sparring with me on the topics covered in this book and for her brutally honest feedback.

My children, MarieSarah (+Chris), EmilyAnne, Andrew (+Adrienne, AnnaBella, and Raelyn), Matthew, and Michael, get special thanks for acting interested in what I am doing.

I mentioned my mom, Carol, in my last book, and she gets thanks again for making me a reader. She is also an avid (and annoying) user of AI.

Then there are the thanks to the mentors mentioned on the dedication page at the front of the book. Tommy Fanning, William Stromberg, Carl Schramm, Steve Renn, Phil Lassiter, Rick Scott, and Guy Sansone. All successful, busy people who took an interest in helping me at different points in my life.

And, of course, there is my wife, Rosanna, who reads each weekly newsletter and book chapter in advance. Her suggested edits are always on point. And yes, she is a better companion than the AIs.

ABOUT THE AUTHOR

George Pillari has appeared on CNN, and been quoted in the *Wall Street Journal*, *New York Times*, and *Washington Post*.

His previous book, *The Seven Deadly Stupidities: Using Other People's Failures to Make Better Decisions*, was an Amazon bestseller.

He publishes a weekly newsletter focused on learning AI at theCautionary.com.

George was an EY Mid-Atlantic Healthcare Entrepreneur of the Year.

As an undergraduate, he co-founded a company with two professors at The Johns Hopkins University. The company grew to more than 1,000 employees, went public, traded on the NASDAQ, and was eventually part of IBM's Watson Artificial Intelligence business.

He has worked as a crisis manager at over 100 companies and was an objective source of truth for a company's board, investors, and lenders.

George has a B.S. in Mathematical Sciences from the Whiting School of Engineering at The Johns Hopkins University.